Nothing Can Stop Me:

An Open Book on Transfer Application Essays

By
Marcie Wald, MSW, LCSW

Foreword By
California State Lieutenant Governor
Cruz M. Bustamante

KENDALL/HUNT PUBLISHING COMPANY
4050 Westmark Drive   Dubuque, Iowa 52002

Copyright © 2005 by Marcie Wald

ISBN 978-0-7575-2183-6

Kendall/Hunt Publishing Company has the exclusive rights to reproduce this work,
to prepare derivative works from this work, to publicly distribute this work,
to publicly perform this work and to publicly display this work.

All rights reserved. No part of this publication may be reproduced,
stored in a retrieval system, or transmitted, in any form or by any
means, electronic, mechanical, photocopying, recording, or otherwise,
without the prior written permission of the copyright owner.

Printed in the United States of America
10 9 8 7 6 5 4 3 2

*This book is dedicated to my heroes,
California community college students.
It is also dedicated to my mentors and friends,
the counselors of Cabrillo Community College.
Both groups maintain dedication
even in the face of constant challenge.*

Table of Contents

FOREWORD III

CHAPTER 1 INTRODUCTION 1

CHAPTER 2 UNIVERSITY OF CALIFORNIA 4

First-Year and Transfer Student Selection 4
    Comprehensive Review 4

Commonalities and Differences Among UC Campuses 5

UC Personal Statement Prompts and Instructions 6
    Question #1 and Rationale: 8
        Prompt 1, Example 1 9
        Prompt 1, Example 2 11
        Prompt 1, Example 3 12
    Question #2 and Rationale: 14
        Prompt 2, Example 1 14
        Prompt 2, Example 2 15
        Prompt 2, Example 3 16
        Prompt 2, Re-entry Scenario 17
    Question #3 and Rationale: 17
        Prompt 3, Example 1 18
        Prompt 3, Example 2 18
        Prompt 3, Example 3 20
        Prompt 3, Example 4 21

Additional Information from UC Interviews 22
    Considerations of the Personal Statement Unique to Transfer Applicants 24
        Choice of Major 24
        Maturity 24
        Omission of Previous Transcripts 25
        The New Merced Campus 25
    Common Strengths in Transfer Student Essays 26
    Common Shortcomings 26
    The Role of the Personal Statements in the Transfer Applicant Selection Process ... 27
    Suggestions Specific to Re-entry Students 30
    English as a Second Language (ESL), Writing Technicalities, and Review 37
        Cohesive Essay or Simple Answer 37
        Review 37
        English as a Second Lanuguage (ESL) 37
        Chart 1: Writing (Paraphrased Responses) 39
        Example of Problematic Writing Quality 43
        General Writing Suggestions 44
    Campus-specific Discussion in Essay Content 45
    Suggestions for Addressing Trauma and Hardship 46
    Discussions of Ethnicity and Other Aspects of Identity That Have Been Targets of Discrimination 48
    A Lack of Out-of-Classroom Experience 49

    Controversial Topics 50
    Writing About Talents and Accomplishments Without Boasting 52
    The Myth of Standing Out 53
    Other Myths and Rumors Reported by UC Admission Professionals 54

Admission by Exception and Letters of Appeal 55

Discussion of Membership in Student Programs 56

Other Sample Essays 56

CHAPTER 3 ESSAYS AND SCHOLARSHIPS 67

Types of UC Scholarships 68

Scholarship Essay Content 68

Other Considerations 70

CHAPTER 4 PRIVATE AND OUT-OF-STATE UNIVERSITIES 71

Private Universities and Four-Year Colleges 71
    University of Chicago 72
    University of Southern California 72
    Santa Clara University 73

Out-Of-State Four-Year Colleges and Universities 74

CHAPTER 5 RECOMMENDED RESOURCES 76

Community College Resources 76

Online and Corporate Resources 76

Printed Resources 78
    General Essay Guidance 78
    Underrepresented Students 79
    University Sources 80
    Writing 81

COMPLETE WORKS CONSULTED 83

ANNOTATED BIBLIOGRAPHY 87

INDEX 97

ACKNOWLEDGEMENTS 104

Foreword

Whether serving as a training ground for millions of our future workers or as a gateway to continued education, community colleges are the building blocks of the State of California's success. For decades, the community colleges have fueled our economic engine and kept our state running strong; and the key factor in maintaining a high level of performance has been the grit and determination of millions of dedicated students.

As you may know, California's community colleges represent the largest system of higher education in the world, serving the needs of approximately 2.9 million students. Our statewide community college system is comprised of 109 schools, divided into 72 different districts.

Community colleges serve an invaluable function in our state by offering affordable skills training and access to higher learning. They boost thousands of hardworking students into better jobs and provide many with the opportunity to earn higher salaries. Educating Californians is the only way that we can expect to continue to be successful in the future.

Our community colleges not only educate our future leaders but also work to power California's unique economy. For every dollar spent at a community college, four dollars may be generated for private and social benefits. Community colleges may produce for local economies anywhere from $3.5 million to $265 million, depending on the size of the district. By helping to educate our population, we are making a wise investment. Two-year colleges have been a significant factor in propelling our Golden State into its position as the sixth-largest economy in the world.

In addition, community colleges act as a critical pathway to California's universities and state college campuses. Last year, community colleges prepared more than 12,000 students to continue their education at a University of California campus, more than 50,000 students to further their training at a California State University campus, and approximately 30,000 students to carry out their studies at private institutions or schools in different states. To assist in their journey, I encourage California community college transfer students to use this guide as an aid in writing with pride about their achievements and experiences as they apply to study at the University of California and private universities in the state.

I have a strong respect for community college students and know from personal experience that they are some of the hardest-working, determined and driven people involved in higher education. Growing up in the small town of Dinuba, in the Central Valley, I quickly realized that to achieve the goals I had set for myself, an education was an absolute necessity. Community college was the best option for me because of the price, the convenience and the close proximity to home. My experience at a two-year school served as a launching pad for the rest of my career. Community college opened countless doors for me and made many of my accomplishments possible.

Each community college student faces his or her own unique challenges and many must also overcome personal and financial hardships. Community college students must be self-motivated to stay on target. The paths students take to realize their dreams are winding and filled with challenges. It is strength of character and steadfast resolve to complete the journey that serves as a common bond among successful California community college students.

I commend those who possess the drive to pursue a higher education. The challenge is difficult and requires intense focus, commitment and hard work. The State of California depends on strong individuals who are prepared to rise to the task.

Cruz M. Bustamante
Lieutenant Governor
State of California
August, 2004

Chapter 1
Introduction

In writing this book, I seek to offer California community college students a broad orientation to the personal statement that addresses considerations distinct from those of high school applicants, for whom plentiful essay-writing guidance is already available. The personal statement is where undergraduate transfer applicants to four-year universities can and should convey the maturity, direction, and varied life experience and achievement that most high school seniors don't yet possess. The content of this book addresses the questions community college students have been asking me during my many years as a community college counselor.

The following story from a community college transfer applicant illustrates one of many ways that adults come to initiate or return to a college education.

> My husband's heart attack threw me back into the work environment...
> My husband needed surgery, we had no income from his business, no health insurance, and it had been over 25 years since I had attended secretarial school. I managed to obtain quick employment on a production line... One day I spotted the president of the company...I gathered up all my courage, stuffed my anxiety in my pocket,...introduced myself, and stated that I had secretarial experience and would like him to review my application. Within two weeks I had secured a position as administrative assistant to a vice president... I took advantage of training seminars and took evening extension courses for 2 years... I slowly advanced to a high profile position working for the chairman of the board of the company...
> (Community College Transfer Applicant to the University of California)

The excerpt above introduces this transfer applicant's personal statement and leads to a discussion of her transfer and career goals. It conveys resilience and dedication through an account that could not possibly have been written by a high school applicant. Although dramatic, stories of sudden life change are not unusual among California's community college population, amongst which more than 442,000 were over 30 years of age in the fall of 2002 (California Postsecondary Education Commission, CPEC). Nor are accounts of the following uncommon:

- The juggling of single parenting, full-time work, and enrollment at the community college
- Intense uncertainty due to being the first in one's family to attend college
- Belatedly discovered learning disabilities

- The need to learn English before fulfilling college level coursework
- Estrangement from family of origin due to history of abuse
- Physical and emotional disabilities
- Poverty and sudden loss of family income
- A degree from another country that is not recognized in the U.S.
- An assortment of college transcripts (often due to military experience)

According to CPEC, approximately 180,000 students transferred from California community colleges to California public universities over the last three years evaluated (2001-2004). A minimum of 8000 community college students transferred to private institutions in the state in the last term that was measured, the fall of 2000. Often, greater competition for transfer seats at the universities, typical in times of budget cuts, increases the importance of the personal statement essay in the selection process. All of the students applying to any University of California (UC) campus, as well as those applying to most private institutions, write application essays.

The most common concern expressed by the transfer students with whom I spoke is a lack of information about the importance of their essays in the universities' selection decisions. Many students wonder about the differences between institutions in the use of their essays and if their statements will even be read. Furthermore, they worry about how to discuss such common issues as poor grades that appeared early in their college records and time taken off from college in order to care for family. Unfortunately, a dearth of information encourages people to fabricate and rely on misleading rumors. The mystique that arises causes widespread anxiety on the part of applicants.

When transfer students begin writing their personal statements and search for models that demonstrate effective discussion of achievements and life circumstances to which they can relate, they are disheartened. In an extensive search of print and online materials, I found only one resource that emphasizes an exploration of the writing of transfer student application essays. In my college's transfer center, I found <u>The Subject is You: Writing the Transfer Essay</u> by Nancy Ginsburg Gil of the Foothill College Writing Center. Unfortunately, this work is not widely distributed or listed in library databases. It contains a number of sample personal statements written by transfer students and focuses predominantly on the writing process itself.

Other essay-related resources target the concerns of high school students applying to exclusive four-year institutions. Such books use essays as examples that usually fail to illustrate the complexity of life circumstances and maturity level common among transfer students. Nor do these books convey the sophistication of transfer students' achievements. Tera Parrett, transfer student, commented on the difference between the personal statement she wrote in high school and the one she wrote as a transfer student, "The essay I wrote as a high school senior is way different from the one I just wrote. My whole outlook has changed. In high school, I had no work experience. I was kind of naive about college. At that time, my perspective was 'what can the university do for me?' Now, I recognize that the university will give me tools to educate myself. And I know that a lot of my education happens outside of the classroom."

Transfer applicants are left with no models from which to draw inspiration and guidance. While some high school students have indeed lived through experiences and accomplishments beyond their years, one admissions dean commented, " From high school seniors we see a lot of stories regarding proms and the acquisition of drivers' licenses. We expect and usually see a different kind of reflection from transfer applicants." This guide provides community college students sample essays to which they can relate and by which they can feel validated.

By drawing from interviews with admissions professionals at each of the UC campuses (with the exception of UC San Francisco, primarily a graduate institution) and at private and out-of-state institutions, with students and others, I intend to add to the meager essay-writing material currently available for transfer applicants, many of whom are associated with groups underrepresented at the university level. The proportion of African-American, Latin-American, Native-American and learning disabled students, as well as students over 25 years of age and single parents is significantly higher in the pool of transfer applicants to four-year institutions than it is in the pool of high school applicants. My book responds to the demographic makeup of California community college transfer students.

Unless I indicate otherwise, I'll be using the phrases "personal statement" and "essay" interchangeably. "Prompt," "question," and "topic" will be used interchangeably as well. "First-year" refers to students applying to a four-year university according to high school eligibility requirements. "Transfer" refers to those who have completed significant lower-division undergraduate coursework (typically 60 semester units) at a college before moving to a four-year institution.

This guide contains a number of actual transfer student essays, in entirety and in parts. All samples are included with the permission of the applicants and are presented on an anonymous basis. Names of people and institutions mentioned in the content of the essays are often omitted or fabricated. Critiques identify strengths as well as ways in which each sample could have been improved. No personal statement can be perfect, so, Transfer Applicant, yours doesn't have to be either.

California community college students, this book is for you. Remember that you have invaluable qualities of your own. As LaRae Lundgren, Director of Undergraduate Admissions, UC Riverside, asserts,

> Due to a generally higher level of maturity, transfer applicants are often better able to describe how life experiences have shaped them and have more life experiences to borrow from.

Write with confidence.

Chapter 2
University of California

First-Year and Transfer Student Selection

With nine, soon ten, campuses, the University of California (UC) absorbs a large number of California community college transfer students: over 180,000 between 2000 and 2003 (CPEC). The criteria and weights used by UC campuses to select first-year college students are usually distinct from those used in the selection of transfer students. As Christian Villasenor, the Assistant Director of Undergraduate Admissions, Transfer Outreach and Articulation, of UC Santa Barbara explains, for transfer students from California community colleges, the best and primary indicator of potential for success at the university level is academic performance during enrollment at the community college. For high school senior applicants, there is no good comparable single indicator of the potential for success at the university. Instead, for first-year applicants, admissions committees need to look at a broader set of factors through a system called comprehensive review.

Comprehensive Review

Under comprehensive review, each first-year application is evaluated according to fourteen categories pre-determined by the UC. Although most of the categories are directly related to academics, a few, such as life experiences that indicate the potential for leadership on a university campus, are not. In addition, some of the academically related criteria, such as the quality of the senior year program, suggest personal attributes such as initiative and curiosity that are often exhibited outside the classroom, too. Personal details included in the essay are part of what informs the assessment of the fourteen criteria. All personal statements of all high school applicants are read. More information about comprehensive review is available through the UC Office of the President, online at <www.ucop.edu>.

In contrast, the personal statement essays play a different role for transfer applicants to most UC campuses. UC Irvine and UC Berkeley are the only campuses that perform a comprehensive review of transfer applications, although UC Merced is hoping to have the staffing to do so as it begins admitting students for the fall of 2005. For most of the UC system, admissions decisions regarding transfer students are based solely on academic performance—specifically, the grade point average (GPA) of UC transferable courses and the completion of required general education courses and courses that prepare applicants for their transfer majors. Consequently, when admissions staff at most campuses read transfer application personal statements, they are in search of information that elaborates on the applicants' academic records. Reviewers commonly look for explanations of aberrations in performance, gaps in enrollment, excess units, and missing coursework. Other, non-academic factors come into play if the academic criteria alone are not able to clarify a decision.

UC admissions professionals usually expect to see clear academic direction from transfer applicants, something they don't expect from first-year applicants. Convincing explanations of the choice of major are often crucial in transfer essays, especially in cases where the applicants' performances are not strong enough to make them clearly eligible for the campus major of their choice. Such explanations can make a difference when admissions staff are choosing between two applicants with similar academic preparation and performance to fill a single opening.

When decision-makers must choose among transfer applicants with comparable academic backgrounds, they may also look for evidence of what the applicants have to offer the campus community or of non-academic indicators of the potential for success. Therefore, discussions of non-academic accomplishments and experience can also be important, even for transfer applicants. Pam Burnett, Director of Undergraduate Admissions at the UC Berkeley campus explains,

> The college community is more complex and heterogeneous than most high school communities. Therefore, leadership roles taken on in that context are more challenging and more of an achievement. Extra commitments while in college demonstrate an even greater ability to handle responsibility. Work achievement, family responsibility *and* progress in higher education demonstrate a deeper commitment to school. The benefit of more life experience and full-time work is enriching in the classroom. It gives applicants a broader range of reference from which to contribute.

Other differences between the role of the essays written by high school and transfer applicants are best explored through noting the distinctions between the practices of the different UC campuses. Additional discussion of such differences follows later in this chapter.

Commonalities and Differences Among UC Campuses

One of the faculty committees of the Academic Senate of the University of California is the Board of Admissions & Relations with Schools. This body oversees admissions policy of the UC system as a whole. However, each campus has its own faculty committee that assures those policies are implemented. The campus committee also has some freedom to determine additional campus-specific policy, such as that relating to the weight of transfer criteria.

Consequently, while there are commonalities, there are also differences in admissions practice and policy among UC campuses. As applicants need to complete only one UC application no matter the number of schools to which they are applying and regardless of the choice of campus, there is only one set of personal statement instructions and prompts. Another commonality is how rarely admissions staff read essays by community college applicants who have completed Transfer Admissions Agreements (TAA's). When these students have specified in their applications that they are also applying for scholarships, their essays *are* read by scholarship committee members. Community college counselors and transfer centers provide information about TAAs. All campuses appreciate seeing signs of direction and explanations of gaps in enrollment in transfer essays. None of the campuses assign differential weight to any of the three personal statement topics. All campuses require that all transfer applicants complete personal statements.

Some campuses read all transfer applicants' personal statements; some do not. Some campuses want transfer applicants to approach the three pieces of the personal statement as they would approach essays or assignments for an English class; some campuses do not want applicants to consider the personal statement as a series of essays, but as straightforward answers to questions, with a focus *entirely* on content. Some of the UCs want applicants to speak to their interest in the campuses of their choice; others discourage this.

Finally, there is variation regarding some issues, such as the significance of grammar in the personal statement and the treatment of controversial themes, among readers at the *same* campus.

The rest of this chapter offers an in-depth exploration of these commonalities and distinctions.

UC Personal Statement Prompts and Instructions

As of the fall of 2003, UC applicants faced a new set of personal statement questions and instructions. Susan Wilbur, Director of Undergraduate Admissions at the UC Office of the President, explained the reasons for the change. Two of the reasons pertained to high school applicants more than to transfers. The previous instructions and prompts were in use before the implementation of comprehensive review for selection of first-year students. The UC wanted to identify new prompts and instructions that would correspond better with this system of review. In addition, admission staff were increasingly alarmed by essays that were written with too much input from, and even content written by, people other than the applicants. It is hoped that the change will reduce the temptation to cheat by making it easier to write the essays.

Other reasons for the newer instructions and prompts apply to all applicants. The UC encourages online application. Ms. Wilbur believes the changes work better with this format. Furthermore, personal statements written according to the former instructions and questions often lacked enough specificity to distinguish one applicant from another. The newer prompts are more targeted and are intended to elicit more descriptive and relevant responses. While applicants must respond to all three prompts, the applicant's choice of the one question to which s/he responds in greater depth offers greater flexibility.

LaRae Lundgren, Director of Undergraduate Admissions, UC Riverside campus says, "I'm excited by the prompts and format. The former two-page statement was effective, but it was somewhat open-ended which, at times, created general statements. Students often didn't know how to focus on what was important. The new rationales give more guidance and focus. But applicants still have the openness of choosing which prompt merits the longer, more in-depth response. The overall length of all three answers is similar to the length of the two-page statement before the change." The inclusion of the rationale for each prompt is entirely new. It is an attempt at both facilitating applicants' understanding and enhancing the probability that admissions professionals find the information they seek.

Susan Wilbur does not expect further changes to the personal statement prompts any time soon. She acknowledges that the results of the new prompts, via an evaluation of the usefulness of up to date personal statements, still need to be assessed. She also asserts that although the effectiveness of prompts is checked regularly, the nature of the information the university needs about transfer applicants is unlikely to change.

The instructions are paraphrased below:

- Respond to all three prompts using a *combined* total of approximately 1000 words
- Limit two responses of your choice to approximately 200 words each
- The third answer to the prompt of your choice should be approximately 600 words in length
- Although each of the three responses is permitted to be a little longer or shorter than the above guidelines, the overall combined total should be as close to 1000 words as possible
- Transfer students must respond to the transfer student prompt under question #1

Applicants are instructed to use the following formatting:

- Use only one side of 8.5" x 11" plain white paper
- Use the 12-point size of a widely known font, such as Times, in black ink or type
- Identify the number of the question you are answering by including the text of the question before your response or by indicating the question number at the start of your answer
- Double-space your response
- Put your name, social security number, and the words "personal statement" at the top of every page

It is extremely important for transfer applicants to follow these instructions. Applicants should avoid making admissions evaluators work any harder than they already must. Evaluators should not be challenged to figure out which question is being answered; even if it is obvious to the writer, it may not be obvious to the reader. Students often groan when they are confronted with a lengthy reading assignment--transfer applicants should pay attention to the visual presentation of their essays to avoid making their readers groan. A statement that has quarter inch margins, for instance, is overwhelming simply because of the large number of words on the page. A standard margin is one inch in width. Applicants should remember that admissions staff are reading hundreds, if not thousands, of essays. Transfer applicant, make it easy for them to read yours.

The UC Gateways web site (<http://www.ucgateways.org>) offers guidance and a tutorial for personal statement writers. The content is directed explicitly at high school senior applicants, but the discussion of the short essay format as well as the preparatory exercises will be useful for some transfer applicants, too. UC Gateways emphasizes that essays should be approached as strategic and persuasive tools. It suggests applicants be prepared to analytically explain why they have made the choices they have made and chosen specific activities. For narrowing down potential topics, it is suggested that an applicant consider which topic best reveals his/her personal reflection and character. UC Gateways highly recommends that applicants choose *one topic* per prompt.

The site also offers specific suggestions for approaching the short essay (200 word) responses. This format does not allow for significant introductions or conclusions. Even though this is a short answer, specific details and examples are still best! No *unnecessary* information should be included, however. It is important to resist the temptation to deal with the word limit by providing lists.

For the longer of the third essay, in contrast, organization of content is more important. Support should be included for main points. It is important for applicants to make sure the reasons why they are sharing the information they are sharing are clear. They should not assume that this will be obvious to their readers.

The UC expects that one essay may be a little under 200 words, for instance, while another may be a little over the guideline. The word count of all three essays combined in the personal statement should not total more than 1000 words, however. The UC will not accept words beyond 630 for the longer essay.

Question #1 and Rationale:

1) Academic Preparation

Rationale: The University seeks to enroll students who take initiative in pursuing their education (for example, developing a special interest in science, language, or the performing arts; or becoming involved in special programs including summer enrichment programs, research or academic development programs such as EAOP, MESA, Puente, COSMOS or other similar programs). This question seeks to understand a student's motivation and dedication to learning.

- Freshman and DAP applicants only: How have you taken advantage of the educational opportunities you have had to prepare for college?
- Transfer applicants only: What is your intended major? Discuss how your interest in the field developed and describe any experience you have had in the field—such as volunteer work, internships and employment, participation in student organizations and activities—and what you have gained from your involvement. (UC Undergraduate Application)

Question #1 distinguishes between freshman and transfer personal statement topics. The UC does not expect applicants from high school to have chosen a major. Transfer applicants, on the other hand, are required to talk about how real experience in the world has brought them to their own choices. The rationale tells us that true and relevant stories that demonstrate initiative, motivation, and dedication to education, or fields of interest, belong in the response to this prompt. Encarnacion Ruiz, Director of Admissions and Relations with Schools and Colleges, of UC Merced, explains the following in relation to question #1:

> The most memorable [statements] are those that explain the foundation of [applicants'] passion and dedication to their major. An example is someone in the military, or a military spouse, who has attended many institutions, taken a variety of classes, changed... focus repeatedly, and then brought themselves to their true and ultimate academic passion. A transfer student's discussion of how this came about often makes for a great statement.

Transfer applicants most often fall short in their answers to question #1 in two ways. First, many students overlook the last phrase of the prompt: "and what you have gained from your involvement." Without addressing this aspect of one's experience, the answer is more likely to seem like a list. A discussion of what one has gained avoids an arrogant tone while elaborating on the experiences themselves. Ignoring what has been gained is a waste of an opportunity to demonstrate a capacity for introspection and make a connection between what one has done, what one is doing and what one will do. To identify experiences in name only is to end the discussion prematurely.

Second, some transfer applicants merely name the internships or jobs they've had and the organizations they've belonged to, but do not *describe* the experiences. Admissions professionals are frustrated when they are given a hint of the applicants' relevant experiences, but aren't given enough information to build pictures of those experiences. If an applicant was involved in student government, it is important to say what post s/he held and describe its responsibilities and the skills it required. An applicant who volunteered should identify the degree of commitment-- a weekend of volunteering? Or was it two years of volunteering for the same organization in increasingly authoritative positions over time? The applicant should also describe tasks completed and skills developed or demonstrated that are relevant to the choice of transfer major. For question #1, only experiences that are relevant to the choice of major should be explored in depth.

Prompt 1, Example 1

The following response to question #1 illustrates effective use of this prompt as an opportunity to reveal relevant and impressive information about oneself.

> The combination of my innate curiosity and opportune life experiences has directed me to my intended major: biology with particular focus on human anatomy and, by extension, comparative anatomy. Since childhood, I have been fascinated by things biological. My initial exposures were informal

and spontaneous. Early on, I was exposed to a wide variety of animals at home, in the veterinary clinic, and assorted animal displays such as parks and aquaria. When I was 7, I dissected a dead gopher snake found by the side of the road with my veterinarian father. Even then I wanted to know what was going on under the skin. My opportunities were limited to observing a few surgeries and the cow's eye dissection at the Exploratorium. Except for a GATE dissection of a cow's heart in 4th grade, most lab experience took place outside of school until I reached college.

My first semester at [community college], I enrolled in Anatomy and Physiology of People. At the time I imagined I was headed for a career as a personal trainer, owing to my fascination with the body and training as a swimmer. Anatomy was my first rigorous college course and my first formal study of the structure and function of the body at the molecular and cellular levels. It changed my life; I was absolutely hooked. I realized that being a personal trainer could in no way match the exhilaration I experienced during lectures and lab. Nor could becoming a trainer justify the sheer intensity of effort it took to be consistently on top of the curriculum. I had found my element, and I recognized that the timing and content of that course would have life-shaping consequences.

The invitation at the end of the course to become Dr. ____'s teaching assistant in the anatomy lab cemented my commitment to the field of study. I continued assisting for seven consecutive semesters, long after I ceased to receive transferable units, and my learning has been ongoing. The lab position deepened my passion and understanding of anatomy while providing me with an outlet for working with people. Reinforcing anatomy and physiology concepts for students in ways they can relate to and witnessing their breakthroughs in understanding simply thrills me. I love being an agent in the learning process, and after 4 years I have reached a personal level of competence and mastery that makes the assignment familiar and easy.

An adjunct benefit of assisting in the lab has been its entrée to participation in 4 dissections at the University's Anthropology Department led by Dr. ____. Over a three-year period I have played a minor role in dissections of an orangutan, gorilla, chimpanzee, and hyena. The project puts anatomical dissection, research, and regard for endangered species in meaningful perspective. Moreover, I am inspired by the work of top women scientists who are applying their knowledge of anatomy and research methods to document and offer insight. The [university] dissections have introduced me to the value and methods of academic research and piqued my interest in exploring further research opportunities in other labs. Specifically, I hope to participate in a biology internship with the 2004 MURF program at Caltech University this summer. I consider myself blessed to have had access to such exceptional learning opportunities. I recognize that interactive skills are important to me, and I expect to pursue science in a context that combines science and communication. Medicine and physical anthropology appeal to me, and a background in biology serves as a good foundation for either venue. Ultimately, I intend to teach anatomy at the college level (Community College Transfer Student Admitted to the UC).

This essay speaks to the rationale behind the question with a number of examples conveying initiative in pursuing educational opportunities, motivation and dedication. Its most important aspect is that it succeeds in answering most of the question. That might seem an easy thing to do, but many admissions professionals complain about how frequently applicants fail to address the prompts. Readers know this student's intended major is biology with an emphasis on anatomy. We know how she cultivated her interest and we know of a number of field-related experiences she has completed.

The introductory paragraph conveys humility through the recognition of having had good opporunities. It also gives an impression of intellectual curiosity. Some readers might question the wisdom of devoting so much space to such early experiences but doing so works for me in this essay.

The second paragraph shows that the applicant is able to self-evaluate and is mature and flexible enough to change plans mid-course. There is some redundancy at its end--it is best to keep the strongest phrases; otherwise, they paradoxically get lost in repetition.

A vote of confidence from an instructor indicates recognition of the student's scholarly nature. The length of the commitment to the role of teaching assistant, and its continuation even after academic credit ran out, suggests dedication and passion. A demonstrated exposure to and interest in research is almost always a plus in the fields of science. The fact that the student is already participating in research at the university level is a benefit. My confidence in the applicant is enhanced by her obvious awareness of what is entailed by study in her chosen field.

Animal research is a controversial topic, but the student relates these experiences to the learning process so consistently that the subject should not be problematic in the selection process. Throughout the essay, the applicant effectively acknowledges what was gained from each educational experience ("The [university] dissections have introduced me to the value and methods of academic research."). Although this student's background is impressive, she succeeds in avoiding an arrogant tone.

Given that most personal statements are reviewed by general admissions staff and not by departmental staff, technical- or field-related abbreviations (G.A.T.E.) should not be used without explanation.

Grammatical errors are few and far between.

Prompt 1, Example 2

The next excerpt also offers a clear discussion of what was gained from an experience relevant to the choice of major.

> I was reassured with my choice to major in Mechanical Engineering when I began working with Professor _____ on her Virtual Reality Machine research project this year. I gained an invaluable learning experience during the course of the project. Designing a simple and easy to manufacture part specific to the project was one of my major

contributions. As I created the part, I realized that the first design is not always the best design. In fact, the machinery needs to be redesigned many times to get as close as possible to perfection. Working with my fellow research partners also gave me the opportunity to enhance my skills in dealing and working with other students and helped me improve my skills in teamwork and compromise. In addition, my ability to communicate ideas was improved last summer when I tutored mathematics at a community college for explaining mathematics to students helped me formulate clearer explanations and relate to others (Community College Transfer Student Admitted to the UC).

Although the writing and punctuation could be improved, the overall paragraph succeeds in identifying what the student gained from participating in the activity described. In addition, it is based entirely on a course-related activity. Such an example demonstrates that even transfer applicants who lack extracurricular experience can write impressive essays.

Prompt 1, Example 3

I like to use the following essay to affirm that it is possible for students to write convincingly even when they lack exceptional career or internship experience.

> Innocent! As a young person, I was fascinated with the debate in the infamous O.J. Simpson murder trial. Sparks flew for me when Marcia Clark cross-examined witnesses and Johnny Cochran convinced the jury not to convict. I was captivated by the case, so much so that I found myself talking about it regularly, and I even sought out different viewpoints of experts through newspaper articles, magazines, and the television. When the climactic verdict was broadcast in my fourth grade classroom, I knew then deep down in my soul that I would one day walk the floor of a courtroom fighting for justice. The seed was planted for my desire to become a prosecuting attorney, and the roots of that seed are growing each day as I continue my quest for a professional law career. At sixteen, I felt that high school classes lacked the challenges that I yearned for. My pursuits and interests were different from those of my peers, as well. On a Friday night, I would rather be home reading a good book, not out "partying." With the support of my family, I went on to graduate high school early. I was excited by the opportunity of attending a local community college and quickly became absorbed in the curriculum. I was given the freedom to explore and excel in many areas of education. I chose to investigate sociology, criminal justice, Italian, and much more. For once in my life, I felt comfortable in my thirst for knowledge. In the midst of my college career, it became clear that I had developed a passion for one particular subject, history.

The class that made the greatest impression on me was "History of the United States prior to 1865." My professor was alive and full of energy. I loved the constant challenge. Weekly quizzes accompanied by lengthy readings were just the beginning of his teachings. I found myself doing whatever it took to succeed in the class. At 7 o'clock in the morning I would be chomping at the bit waiting for the library doors to open so that I could begin researching "the shot heard around the world." Being successful in this class made me realize that I will be able to handle the research required in my future legal career.

I became very involved in the class by hosting a dynamic study group. I took the opportunity to create packets of information I had researched and design pretests to prepare the group for examinations. I realized that at seventeen I was leading a group of adults in exciting, intense, and wonderful debates and discussion, two to three times per week. I received great pleasure employing leadership skills that I will use as an attorney. I now have the ability to b e productive out of class as well as in class, strength to work cooperatively and independently, and a growing passion for learning more of the experiences of our forefathers and of the people of other cultures in our world.

Through my community college career, I have gained the insight that specializing in history will be my goal during my undergraduate education. If I am going to fight for justice in the future, I need to have a knowledgeable foundation of our past! To understand any historical event requires understanding what preceded it, just as law uses precedence. I have found that I simply love the subject of history, and I am really looking forward to broadening that knowledge. As a major, I believe that it will be the perfect step to achieving my ultimate goal of becoming an attorney (Community College Transfer Applicant to the UC).

Although graduating high school and entering college early is exceptional, this detail is not what makes this essay impressive. Indeed, even with the second paragraph removed, I would find this essay persuasive.

Some readers might appreciate the examples of educational dedication during high school as a relevant demonstration of passion. I find it, as well as the list of college subjects studied, unnecessary. The writer could have mentioned more concisely the early completion of high school to start college and then moved directly to the transition, "In the midst of my college career, it became clear that I had developed a passion for one particular subject, history."

The details that are most compelling are the search for different viewpoints and use of various media even at a young age; the grasp of the analogy between history and precedence; and the initiative, resourcefulness, determination, and leadership demonstrated by creating a study group and corresponding materials. The student does not forget to describe what she gained from her experience.

This essay is not superbly written, but is written well enough. Readers are able to gain a sense of the students' motivation and dedication (as requested by topic #1's rationale) even though the primary experience discussed is one that most community college students could create for themselves.

Question #2 and Rationale:

Potential to Contribute
Rationale: UC welcomes the contributions each student brings to the campus learning community. This question seeks to determine an applicant's academic or creative interests and potential to contribute to the vitality of the University.

- Tell us about a talent, experience, contribution or personal quality you will bring to the University of California. (UC Undergraduate Application)

This prompt is the same for first-year and transfer applicants. Many transfer applicants, however, have broader life experience from which to draw in their responses. Many refer to talents they exhibited in previous careers or personal qualities they manifested in the context of helping to support their families—logistically, financially, or emotionally.

One of the more frequent weaknesses that appear in prompt #2 essays is, again, a lack of description complete enough to communicate thoughtfulness and depth. Unfortunately, the potential for answering this question with a list is high because so many students want to convey multi-dimensionality and do so by emphasizing quantity instead of quality of experience. Even applicants who do have a variety of talents and qualities should focus on the one or two that are most relevant to a university community. Remember, the prompt instructs applicants to speak about *one*!

An additional caution pertains to the temptation to write this portion of the statement with a focus on someone else. Applicants hope that writing about their mentors reveals information about themselves by virtue of their admiration. One admissions director refers to this as the "grandmother syndrome": "Gee, we'd love to admit your grandma! But what are *you* like?" This happens more in essays written by first year applicants, but transfer students sometimes make this mistake, too.

Some applicants attempt to address the vitality mentioned in the rationale by restating their contribution or talent with the use of effusive and redundant vocabulary instead of by illustrating how that talent or quality has been verified by experience.

Prompt 2, Example 1

The following quote represents the majority of a full response to prompt #2.

> Everyone knows that not everyone is the same. Not everyone is a math genius or a star athlete. Everyone has their strengths and weaknesses. For example, some people are better at writing poems, while others are better at working out math problems. Wether, it is a school subject, a sport, or playing an instrument, everyone has a strength. I am strong in math. I love working with numbers. In high school I took six years of math. My talent

is talking to people. I am a total people's person. (Community College Transfer Student Admitted to the UC)

The rest of the answer continues in the same vein. Sadly, the first five sentences reveal nothing about the applicant. Instead, they attempt to teach the admissions staff something about the world. This is not an appropriate use of any component of the personal statement. Further, these lines waste a precious opportunity to reveal something impressive about the writer herself.

This student declares two strengths: math and social interaction. Although she reasserts her passion for these activities with repetitious claims, she does not describe with plausible detail how she has demonstrated these talents. Reiterating claims of a personal quality does not validate those claims--readers don't take the applicants' word for it. A description of how that quality has been displayed in a constructive way is more influential. The closest this applicant gets to a concrete detail that supports her claim is her reference to six years of high school math. For transfer students who have been attending community college, examples from life after high school are far more persuasive. But even in this mention of high school, the writer does not discuss her success in these courses, the highest level achieved, or her favorite branch of math. Unfortunately, the poor grammar and few misspellings do not help redeem this essay.

Prompt 2, Example 2

The prompt #2 essay that comes next provides sufficient evidence of the personal quality claimed by the writer.

> The greatest personal asset I would bring to the campus learning community is extensive cross-cultural experience that has led to a deep level of respect for diversity. Growing up in Vietnam in the 70's and 80's, I did not have much contact with other cultures. But when I became a translator and began to interact with the international business community, I was immediately exposed to people from a broad range of backgrounds: Australian, American, French, Malaysian, Chinese, British, and Indian. Then my social life became naturally immersed in the ex-patriot community of Hanoi. The experiences of working with and then becoming friends with people from other national, religious and cultural traditions broadened my mind and gave me the ability to really appreciate how much each of us are a product of our own backgrounds. I have since been fortunate to live and work with H'mung hill tribe people, to learn to love one sister-in-law who is gay and another who is a fundamentalist orthodox Jew! I now have dear friends all over the world – even in Tuva! I strongly believe that the deep, natural interest in other's traditions and perspectives these experiences have awoken in me will be my greatest asset in the UC learning community. (Community College Transfer Student Admitted to the UC)

Many people claim multi-cultural awareness but are not convincing in their discussions of that awareness. This writer's exposure to other cultures comes from extensive practical experience. She recognizes that culture is not only a matter of geography but of other variables such as religion and sexual orientation. That this student has sought out working with people from diverse cultures, including remote ones, and entwined her social life with that of an ex-patriot community, shows an authentic receptivity to and comfort level with those who are different. It is the sum of the details that make this a persuasive statement. Unfortunately, this person does not spell out *how* her interest in diverse cultures will be an asset in the UC learning community. Such an addition would have made this response even more powerful.

Prompt 2, Example 3

In almost every essay workshop I have conducted, some transfer students have expressed doubt that they have something compelling to write about. They lament, "I've never been in a debilitating car accident, recovered from a drug problem or had a husband who had a heart attack!" Admissions professionals tell me that personal statements are adequately compelling if they simply accomplish conveying an authentic voice and the information requested.

A look at another #2 essay, written by an aspiring teacher, helps make this point.

> Outside the classroom, I enjoy working out, swimming, art projects and playing music. For years, swimming has been a metaphor for persisting when things are difficult and going beyond inner barriers. Fortunately, my teachers had confidence in me when I lacked confidence in myself. They had the wisdom and patience to allow me to develop as a swimmer at my own pace. In the end, I emerged a swimmer with form, strength, and confidence. For 3 seasons I returned to teach a new generation of novices. I value having had the experience of transforming resistance into mastery. By comparison, music has been effortless. I began learning the flute in 4th grade and have continued privately ever since. Through the years, my teacher has expanded my exposure to include clarinet, oboe, guitar and viola da Gamba. Art has also been an outlet. Except for a single semester of hand-built ceramics, my art projects have been informal and part of my life since childhood. The ceramics class was remarkably inspiring, and I felt stimulated by all the creative energy around me. I flourished in the non-judgmental and supportive environment. I appreciate having a variety of interests to remind me that I am multi-dimensional (Community College Transfer Student Admitted to the UC).

Clearly, this student wanted to convey multi-dimensionality. Ironically, the second part of the response reads so much like a list that it dilutes the powerful impressions left by the first part about swimming. The mentions of music and art do not add significantly to a broader picture of the applicant. This essay would have been stronger with the second half omitted. Or, the student could have given the brief list of interests in the first sentence, and then used the rest of the 200 words to underscore how qualities exemplified in the swimming story apply at a university campus. Remember, the most universal advice is to go into depth about one or two talents or accomplishments rather than saying less about entries on a longer list. Although the swimming-as-a-metaphor sentence is a bit awkward, the swimming section as a whole conveys a great deal of impressive information about this applicant.

First, we see that this student is able to credit others and accept input. This suggests self-awareness and a capacity for teamwork in any number of contexts. An involvement of at least four years is a good sign of commitment and persistence. The instructional experience referenced here supports the applicant's claim of teaching as a career goal. The concept of transforming resistance into mastery is sophisticated, relevant to teaching, and descriptive. And the concept is conveyed with the use of only a few words! Even though the swimming story is not dramatic or extraordinary, it is sufficiently compelling.

This student had the chance to cull from the story a number of personal attributes that would be of value at a university. At times this was done; at times I had to read between the lines. Further, the writer stopped short, as so many applicants do, of bridging this story to a vision of being a member of a university community.

Prompt 2, Re-entry Scenario

Some re-entry students who spent the bulk of their time as homemakers while away from school express concern that they have no talent, experience, personal quality, or contribution to bring to the university. I asked UC admission staff about this issue. Lena Brown, Student Affairs Officer, Transfer Recruitment, of the UC Los Angeles Admissions Office sums up the perspective that homemakers should keep in mind:

> Homemakers should discuss what they did as homemakers. Often they spend time at the kids' schools, PTA, church, volunteering, making time for other family members. This definitely demonstrates scheduling, time-management, multi-tasking, and juggling skills also necessary for success at the university.

Volunteering and spending time at the kids' schools most likely require a variety of other skills as well. Supervisory, event planning, public speaking, and diplomatic skills are a few that come to mind. A transfer student who has spent many years overseeing a house full of teenagers, for example, might make the case that he could contribute to the university by being a resident assistant in a dormitory.

The key to a successful discussion of this kind is, again, relevant description instead of lists. Only via a foundation in description can the writer plausibly name personal qualities. Of course, the writer should then explain how these personal qualities are relevant in the context of a university campus.

Question #3 and Rationale:

> "Open-ended"
> This question seeks to give students the opportunity to share important aspects of their schooling or their lives—such as their personal circumstances, family experiences and opportunities that were or were not available at their school or college—that may not have been sufficiently addressed elsewhere in the application.

- Is there anything you would like us to know about you or your academic record that you have not had the opportunity to describe elsewhere in this application? (UC Undergraduate Application)

Prompt 3, Example 1

The next transfer student's story is an appropriate response to prompt #3.

> I think it is important to mention that I was admitted to UC ____ for the fall of 2000, through the early academic outreach program, guaranteed admission from high school. However, I was not able to take advantage of this opportunity at that time. I am the youngest of three daughters and we have been a large financial responsibility for my mother. Currently, our financial situation is stable, but it has not always been this way. It was mostly due to finances that I decided to delay my enrollment with a four-year university until now. My oldest sister moved to attend veterinary school during my senior year of high school and as a family we were trying to help her though school. She has since returned with her degree and it is now my turn to focus on my education. I would also like to mention that during my last few years at the community college, I have been working to help financially around the house and help myself through school. However, my work hours and wages would not always allow me the funds to purchase all of the necessary required reading and my grades reflect this (Community College Transfer Student admitted to the UC).

The reader is informed, in a straightforward manner, that this student faced family and financial responsibilities that affected her educational decisions and performance. Just as important, she follows up that point by assuring the university that the situation is different now and she can commit fully to study at the university level. Unfortunately, the writer leaves herself vulnerable in her excuse for not completing all reading assignments because readers know that most required reading is accessible via school libraries.

Prompt 3, Example 2

This applicant also appropriately uses question #3 for supplemental comments:

> Additional Comments
>
> I was not able to list my awards on section 6 … the computer kept giving me error messages related to the dates as I entered them. I believe that I entered them correctly as such: Dean's list at the community college fall of 2002, 2003. Academic recognition for a High School GPA above 3.5 June 2000. Coaches and participation award for Volleyball Fall of 1996, 1997, 1998. Work experience: I have worked as a Veterinary Technician for the past 5 years. My hours have ranged from part-time while in school to full-time when not. My responsibilities included monitoring anesthesia,

helping with surgery, giving vaccines and speaking to clients about important decisions involving the health care of their animals. I would like to put my earnings toward education and my family responsibilities.

Many of the details of the same student's answer to question #2 belong in the response to question #3.

I think that I will bring a distinctive perspective of higher education in the United States of America to the UC.... This perspective is unique in some ways, but similar to other young immigrants in others. I want to be successful (like other young immigrants), but I want to achieve my success through education. This idea was born from exposure. My mother, my father, my two older sisters and myself immigrated to the United States from...Columbia in the mid 1980's. We were faced with the hardships of a typical immigrant family, language barriers, culture barriers, etc., and it was during these difficult times, that I witnessed my mother's struggle for our progress. My mother worked full-time, attended college full-time, and raised three daughters full-time. My father left and returned to Columbia when we were still very young, and without any other family in the United States, we solely depended on my mother's efforts. My family and I were homeless for a year. During this time, we survived the streets of South Central Los Angeles, we bounced from homeless shelter to homeless shelter, but throughout this entire time my mother continued to attend school. I saw the difference in our lives as my mother was able to speak English, when she got an AA degree, when she received her B.S. degree, when she received her teaching credentials and finally her Master's degree. I have lived the difference and it is this experience that drives me to pursue further education. I would like to achieve my goals, as my mother even in the face of hardship. I would like to secure my future with education, as I have seen my mother do. I am a strong believer in education as a means to a successful life. I have seen my mother's progress and most recently witnessed my oldest sister's graduation as a Doctor of Veterinary Medicine from ---University. It was also hard work and commitment that allowed my sister to take full advantage of the opportunities presented in education and which have lead her to a successful life. I plan to obtain a B.A. degree and continue my education toward a PhD, eventually returning the favor and teaching another generation. I think that my commitment to education is evident based on my experience and I would like to convey this enthusiasm to others. I feel that as part of the UC _____ campus I would use this experience as a tool for encouragement and drive. Although everyone's college experience is their own and is whatever they make it, I feel that having people like myself would help create a better learning atmosphere. I am motivated to learn, eager to help others, and although I am still very young, I am ready to make education my priority. I have taken a year off from school in order to save some money to be prepared for this commitment. I hope that you agree with me in that I would make a positive addition to the current UC.... I feel that my distinctive background would give me some insight into what it takes to have a successful education. I would like to take the opportunity to benefit from the example that my mother and my sister have set and make it my own. I would also like to mention that although I have placed a great amount of importance on the basic idea of higher education, I cannot forget to mention my interest in the psychology field, personally, I always find it interesting to speak to people that are informed about psychology.

Although this transfer student does reiterate her belief that her contribution would be the high value she places on education, an appropriate topic for prompt #2, most of the description she provides is about challenges or other people. She does have to provide enough details of her family's struggle to convey the factors that honed her perspective on education. However, the statement would have been easier to follow and more powerful if she had separated into distinct essays the topics of adversity she and her family overcame (and how they overcame it) and that of her potential to contribute to the campus community. By combining these conversations in one essay, her own promise of contributing is overshadowed by family members' achievements. She lacks specificity regarding *how* she would use her academic dedication to help others, such as through tutoring or serving as a peer counselor for students who come from an immigrant background.

Given that this student's academic history was influenced by her family's struggles against significant obstacles, the high degree of detail fits best with the rationale of question #3. Wisely, this applicant includes discussion about her role in the family's struggles. The details paint a picture that evokes admiration and understanding. The mention of psychology at the end, however, is unnecessary. At times the writing could be stronger, but this is not enough of a problem to take away from the effect of the content as a whole.

Prompt 3, Example 3

An excerpt from another transfer applicant's response to question #3 provides an interesting contrast to the previous essay.

> The support of my family has been the biggest inhibitor of my academic success. I am the first person in my family to go to college, which explains the low level of support provided by my immediate family. My family understands the importance of college and has always held that I would be the "one" to go to college, but they have never fully understood what my success entails on their part. Due to my mother's single income and 2 other children to provide for, financial support for college was not provided. This translated into my mother and grandfather suggesting that I should drop out school or move back home because I am constantly in a financial strain, both of which I have tried to no avail. The first option of living at home while in college did not work because my family could not comprehend the level of home studying required in college. As a result,

while living at home I had no time to study. Instead, my time was spent helping my sisters with homework, completing housework, or cooking meals while my mother worked overtime. I also worked multiple jobs, often over forty hours a week, while attempting to carry a full course load. I am grateful that I have remained in school, despite the physical, financial, and familial pressures I continue to endure and I look forward towards my future as a college graduate (Community College Transfer Applicant to the UC).

The strengths of this paragraph include that it gives description detailed enough to convince the reader that there was, indeed, a lack of support from the family significant enough to compromise the student's success. It also shows that the applicant is dedicated to her education enough to persist by attempting a variety of solutions.

The paragraph could have been made stronger with some changes. The quality of the writing itself could have been stronger, including more careful wording of the first sentence (the *limits* of her family's support is the inhibitor of success). In addition, a more positive and promising tone could have been conveyed with some discussion of how this student intends to minimize such challenges while studying at the university—has she been saving money so that she won't have to work so many hours? Has her family gained in understanding of the demands inherent in college study?

Although the families of both applicants provide differing degrees of support and understanding, the applicants in both examples have faced socioeconomic challenges. The first applicant, however, attempts to reassure admissions staff that she has a plan that will keep such struggles from interfering in her university studies. The applicant in the second example leaves this issue in question.

Prompt #3 is open-ended by design, but applicants should bridge all responses to some aspect of their education. When the response is an explanation of a rough episode in one's past, it is suggested that the bulk of the essay focus on how the trouble was overcome and on evidence that it will not be a problem for the student at the university.

Michael Dang, Associate Director of UC Davis' Undergraduate and Outreach Services, offers a unique perspective on circumstances in which applicants fail to take advantage of the opportunity that prompt #3 gives to them:

> There can be a problem when people *don't* acknowledge when a trauma influenced a very obvious dip in grades. A lack of explanation for the poor section of the transcripts doesn't help these students. When the explanation is there, it's important to follow through with a discussion of how the writer coped or is coping with the trauma. More of the space should be devoted to that response and not so much to the details of the trauma.

Prompt 3, Example 4

Transfer students who *haven't* experienced extraordinary hardship often ask about how they can make use of prompt #3. The essay presented next references hardship, but not extreme or even uncommon hardship. It also allows the applicant to share a story not directly relevant to university study but a story that, nevertheless, reveals personal qualities that help readers understand the applicant as a whole person. Also note that a positive tone is established from the beginning.

> I grew up in a single parent family with a wonderful father. We had limited resources and my mother was not in the picture. Even though, there were limitations on what my father could provide, he did share with me the art of surfing. I learned to surf from an early age and simply loved it.
>
> Through this sport, I have become connected with my community. One focal person that has entered my life is Cathy. Cathy took me under her wing as her child and gave me a sense of security. She showed me how surfing can keep me grounded and centered. One time when we were surfing, she shared with me how to do the best with what I have in any situation. Cathy, along with many other surfers, has become the family I never had.
>
> The influence of these people has given me the confidence to be a competitive surfer and win, the ability to find willing sponsors, and the commitment to never give up. I also now have the heart to give back by volunteering my skills in local organizations that give children and adults with disabilities a chance to experience and enjoy the ocean (Community College Transfer Applicant to the UC).

The weakest section of this essay is the discussion of the time that Cathy "shared with me how to do the best with what I have in any situation." If this was a one-time exceptional piece of advice, we, the readers, want in on it. Such wisdom is usually modelled or taught over time. This section is especially awkward in its writing.

The final paragraph, however, conveys an appealing dimension to the applicant. I believe this applicant is a "winner" in life, and even moreso because she has the generosity to share her sea-loving spirit with those who might otherwise find the ocean inaccessible.

Additional Information from UC Interviews

In an effort to research the issues that transfer applicants wonder about in relation to their personal statements for the UC, I interviewed an admissions professional at each of the UC campuses (with the exception of San Francisco, primarily a graduate institution) during the Fall of 2003 and Winter of 2004. The rest of this chapter details the information given to me during those interviews.

UC Professionals Interviewed, 2003-4

Interviewee	*Title*	*Affiliation*
Susan Wilbur	Director of Undergraduate Admissions	UC Office of the President
Pamela L. Burnett	Director, Office of Undergraduate Admissions	Berkeley
Robert F. Giomi	Assistant Dean, College of Engineering	Berkeley
Michael Dang	Associate Director, Undergraduate Admissions and	Davis

	Outreach Services	
Marguerite Bonous-Hammarth, PhD.	Director, Admissions & Relations with Schools	Irvine
Lena Brown	Student Affairs Officer, Transfer Admissions	Los Angeles
Encarnacion Ruiz	Director, Admissions/Relations with Schools & Colleges	Merced
Susan Fauroat	Associate Director, Admissions/Relations with Schools & Colleges	
Lori Jones	Outreach Coordinator	
LaRae Lundgren	Director, Undergraduate Admissions	Riverside
Nathan Evans	Associate Director, Admissions & Relations with Schools	San Diego
Christian Villasenor	Assistant Director, Undergraduate Admissions, Transfer Outreach and Articulation	Santa Barbara
Michael McCawley	Associate Director, Office of Admissions	Santa Cruz

I asked open-ended questions to elicit as much information as possible.

- What considerations of the admission essays are unique to transfer students? What should the essays convey about a transfer student that they don't need to convey about a first-year applicant?
- What are the most common shortcomings you see in transfer student essays? Are there strengths you see in essays from transfer applicants that you see less often in essays from first-year applicants?
- What is the role of the transfer essays in the university selection process? What is the weight given to the essays? Does the weight vary by major?
- Who at the university reads the essays--general admissions staff or faculty in the major or department?
- Who at the university makes the selection decisions? How are those decisions made? What is the process?
- Do you have any suggestions specifically for re-entry students? Some people who were primarily homemakers during their time away from school express concern about how to discuss that time. Do you have any suggestions?
- How important is it for the writing to be grammatically correct?
- Some English as a Second Language (ESL) students express concern that they are at a disadvantage in writing the essays, even if they have succeeded in their college level English composition classes, because they are not as fluent in English. Do you have any comment on this?
- Is the longer essay weighed more heavily than the shorter ones?
- Writing instruction often places emphasis on the introductory and concluding paragraphs and topic sentences. Are these significant in the personal statements?

- Is it important for students to explain why they are applying to your campus?
- Do you have suggestions for effectively addressing past traumas and hardships? Students fear their discussion will be interpreted as emotional manipulation. What do you think?
- Some students fear that their essays will have less impact and that they will be at a disadvantage if they have not overcome a hardship of some kind. What is your response?
- Some students have not had much out-of-classroom experience. Given that it is too late to get significant experience that can be referenced in their personal statements, what is your advice for conveying a positive impression?
- What is your opinion about having a variety of people review applicants' essays before submission?
- How should applicants discuss controversial opinions relevant to the theme of the essays? Or should applicants avoid controversial themes altogether?
- How would you characterize the difference between ineffective boasting and effective acknowledgment of one's achievements and talents?
- I advise students not to emphasize creativity, originality, or humor if doing so is at the expense of communicating important information about themselves. Is this appropriate guidance?
- What are myths and rumors about the essay portion of the application and selection process that applicants should ignore?

Considerations of the Personal Statement Unique to Transfer Applicants

Choice of Major

"The application statement is very different for transfer than first year applicants. The assumption for transfers is that they are focused on their major. [Transfer applicants] should speak of their interest in their field...They should explain unique life experiences that influenced their records." Michael Dang of UC Davis

This book has already begun exploring this perspective, but there is more to add. Especially helpful in the statements is content that conveys that the applicants truly understand what is entailed in the study of their chosen fields. Occasionally, an essay communicates that an applicant has an unrealistic view, or no view at all, of the path to his/her own goal. This problem most frequently occurs in statements written for majors that lead to high status, high wage careers. The applicants may be so attached to the perceived rewards of the end goal that they disregard the reality of the work required to get there. The discussion of the choice of major is even more important for engineering and science majors because there is usually fierce competition for admission to these majors and there is a higher attrition rate due to the challenging nature of the curriculum.

Maturity

The maturity of transfer applicants is communicated through stories that demonstrate some combination of initiative, introspection, receptivity to challenges, self-awareness, responsibility, assertiveness, self-reliance, resourcefulness, resilience, and commitment. However, all admissions professionals are in agreement that most important is the authenticity of the writers' voices. Transfer students, then, must be careful not to fabricate or stretch material in the essay for the sake of sounding good. When a reviewer reads hundreds or thousands of statements, the distinction between a sincere and unique voice and a contrived one is blatantly apparent.

Omission of Previous Transcripts

The omission of portions of academic history is problematic enough that admissions readers actively look for explanations of time periods for which transfer students have provided no records. Although the application clearly states that all applicants must report *all* schools attended after high school, many transfer students persist under the misconception that some circumstances excuse them from this requirement. Typically, if a student attended one community college years ago and earned poor grades in courses they have subsequently repeated elsewhere, s/he thinks the earlier transcripts are not relevant and not required. This also happens when students "hardly completed any courses" at previous community college.

Michael McCawley of UC Santa Cruz, is adamant about this issue.

> Unfortunately, every year there are a number of cases of withholding of information and/or falsification of academic history. This often happens when re-entry students act on the belief that an earlier time in their history that doesn't reflect who they currently are... "doesn't count." Therefore, they choose not to include those records. This is a terrible mistake. Don't do this! Such omission or deception is often discovered and consequences are severe! It has happened that someone was barred from UCSC and the UC system as a whole, *just before graduation*...for such withholding....The UC system now does system-wide verifications. UCSC [alone] usually sees six to eight cases a year like this.

In some cases, the students don't submit all transcripts at the time of application because doing so would give them too many units for admission to some campuses. Then, in their senior years, they submit the missing transcripts to their advisors because they need specific units to fulfill specific requirements. Cases of omission or deception are often discovered through financial aid records, as well.

Clearly, this is an issue specific to transfer students. It pertains to personal statements because admissions workers seek out discussions in the statements that will convince them that applicants are accounting for all of their time since high school.

The New Merced Campus

The new UC Merced campus is in a unique position as it will be building a campus community from the moment of enrollment of its first students. The campus is scheduled to open in the Fall of 2005. According to Encarnacion Ruiz, UC Merced, administrators had the option of waiting to admit transfer students until a later term, after the campus had established a foundation with recent high school graduates. Instead, they decided to admit transfer students from the beginning because they recognized that transfer students have something distinct to offer in the creation of a university community. Transfer students will play an active role in the birth and development of student committees, clubs, and governance.

Given that UC Merced will need students who are innovative, take chances, can fill leadership roles and draw from initiative, the involvement of transfer students will be invaluable. In addition, UC Merced will at first have only a small pool of graduate students from which to draw research assistants so, at first, undergraduate students will have a rare opportunity to gain research experience usually conducted only by graduates. Transfer applicants to UC Merced should bear all of this in mind when choosing which experiences to discuss in their personal statement essays.

The selection of the students that will compose the first student body at UC Merced will have so much influence on the campus that it will involve an extra degree of complexity. Consequently, it is likely that all transfer applicant essays will be reviewed. Campus-specific guidelines are still being identified with the input of faculty.

Common Strengths in Transfer Student Essays

There is no better way to describe the strengths most often seen in the personal statements of transfer applicants than to make known the comments of UC admissions administrators. When Christian Villasenor, UC Santa Barbara, summarizes strengths specific to the personal statements of transfer applicants, he articulates a message I heard from most of the admissions professionals with whom I spoke:

> Transfer students usually have a better idea of where they're going and what they want to do regarding a major and career goals. Their claims are often more believable because of more extensive real world life experience. Transfer students are more likely to reference research experience and interests. They are occasionally familiar with the work of faculty at the UC.

Nathan Evans of UC San Diego, added the following:

> Transfer applicants often convey a better understanding of higher education environments and tools and resources necessary for success. They also often convey an ability to recognize their own weaknesses and how they have overcome or compensated for them.

UC Los Angeles' Lena Brown had this to say. "…The transfer students' discussions generally show thoughtfulness about life choices and decisions more than seniors' discussions do."

Of course, there is room for improvement as well.

Common Shortcomings

By far, the shortcoming most commonly named is the lack of detailed, descriptive content. It is important for applicants to *develop*, with examples, their most important points. Interest and motivation should be shown, not simply claimed. In addition, failing to respond to the prompts or ignoring the choice of major in the body of the personal statement can mean the difference between securing a coveted spot among the admitted and being denied that spot.

Even in regard to academic preparation and history, detailed explanations can be important. Encarnacion Ruiz of UC Merced gives this example. "Do the transcripts show an absence of any college level math class? If so, an explanation is necessary—did the applicant place into college level math via assessment and therefore need only one math class?" Students in this situation should not wait until their last term at the community college to take the one math class required for admission, but if they do, they must realize the transfer institutions to which they are applying are initially looking at transcripts that show that a basic requirement is missing. Even the level of detail that offers a plausible explanation for something as specific as the absence of one math class should be included in the personal statement if it is relevant to eligibility for admission.

Christian Villasenor of UC Santa Barbara identified another shortcoming.

> Too much about external sources of inspiration, especially about family role models, and not enough about themselves. We end up thinking, 'Wow! We'd love to admit your grandma!' [Applicants] shouldn't waste their 'interview' talking about other people. [They should] think of the personal statement as a substitute for an interview. If referencing someone else as an inspiration, [they should] make sure to quickly bring the focus back to themselves.

Given that some cultures do not recognize "self" as separate from family or discourage a focus on self more than on family, this can be challenging for many applicants. For many, describing family hardships and achievements is the same thing as describing their own. In these cases, it is a stretch to have to distinguish themselves from family members in any way. Yet, the task of conveying their own potential to contribute, plans, and strengths remains.

Finally, unexplained gaps in educational histories or aberrations are a potentially pivotal shortcoming. This will be explained in more detail later in this chapter.

The Role of the Personal Statements in the Transfer Applicant Selection Process

I can safely make only a few generalizations about the role and weight of the essays in the selection process. No specific weight is assigned to transfer applicant essays. The statements alone are not scored or rated. The personal statements are never as significant as the transferable GPA, minimum unit and course requirements for admission, and lower-division preparation for the transfer major. Essays that accompany applications of students with approved Transfer Admission Agreements (TAA's) are rarely read by admissions personnel. They are, however, read by scholarship committees if applicants have expressed interest in scholarships. Transfer essays are most often reviewed in search of explanations and justifications of exceptional periods, poor performance, and substitutions in academic histories. Schools of Engineering often conduct their own application reviews, using both faculty and administrators.

Other issues are complex enough and vary so greatly by campus, they are best explained through paraphrasing the admissions professionals with whom I spoke.

I asked these questions of each admission professional:

- What is the role of the essays in the selection process?
- What is the weight given to the essays?
- Who at the university reads the essays?
- Who makes the selection decisions?
- How are those decisions made?
- What is the process?

Emphasis is mine in the following paraphrased responses. Italics call attention to less common perspectives.

UCB, Pam Burnett

A poorly written essay is a waste of an opportunity for the College of Letters & Science (L&S). A strong essay is a good addition to the application packet, but doesn't necessarily mean the person will be admitted. No specific weight is given to transfer essays. General admissions staff read the essays *as part of a comprehensive review of each transfer application. Each application as a whole is rated.* Selections are made according to target numbers for each program. At other colleges, faculty and administrative staff read the applications and make the selection decisions. The weight of the essays is greater at some of the other colleges.

UCB, College of Engineering (COE), Bob Giomi

At the COE, the personal statement is an important way to distinguish between applicants with similar academic preparation and grade point averages (G.P.A.s.) *The weight varies by engineering major.* For transfer applicants, general admissions staff screen by GPA per engineering major. Then, the whole application, including the personal statement, is read by one staff member from the Dean's Office and one faculty member from the major department. *The application is scored by each person separately and then passed on to the college's adjudicator by whom the final decision is made.*

UCD, Michael Dang

The essay is a supportive document. *Not all transfer applicant personal statements are read.* If students are clearly eligible, whether the essays are read or not depends on the applicant pool for the desired major. More weight is given to the essays in cases of borderline eligibility. Other than for the COE, general admissions staff read the applications and make the decisions. An initial group is screened out. *Remaining applications receive a full evaluation. Transfer applications are not scored or given points.* In selective majors, admissions staff check for lower division major preparation. General admissions staff do the initial preparation of the applications for the COE. Then COE faculty and administrators do their own evaluations. *The essays carry more weight and can help compensate for missing lower division requirements.*

UCI, Marguerite Bonous-Hammarth, Ph.D.

Personal Statements are used as a complement to the rest of the record. Personal statements are not weighted. Major preparation is weighed heavily. *Faculty and counselors are readers along with general admissions staff.* UCI does a comprehensive review of transfer students' applications so all personal statements are read. The selection process is computer-assisted.

UCLA, Lena Brown

The personal statements are read primarily for explanations of aberrations in the academic history. General admissions staff read the applications and make the admission decisions for most majors. *In the majors of Nursing, Communication Studies, Engineering, and Arts and Television, faculty read the applications and make the selection decisions* after an initial screening by general admissions staff. No outside readers are used for transfer applications. Initial evaluations are completed first, then the essays are looked at during the second read-through of applications.

UCM, Encarnacion Ruiz, Susan Fauroat, and Lori Jones

The process has yet to be determined with faculty input. The Faculty Committee on Admissions and Outreach will draw up selection criteria. We intend and hope for faculty involvement in the reading of applications. Admissions and Outreach staff will review the applications and personal statements. There may be outside readers as well. We hope to have the resources to read all transfer applicant essays. Some parts of the application can only be fairly evaluated by a human being, so while there may be some computer assistance in the review of applications, mostly due to a shortage of staff, professional admissions staff will complete the bulk of the work.

UCR, LaRae Lundgren

UCR does not implement comprehensive review for transfer applications at this time. Staff read essays if they need an explanation of something in the record. No weight is given to the statement itself. For most majors, admissions staff read the essays. Each application is assigned to an admissions counselor. *A computerized auto-admit program checks for minimum UC eligibility. An admissions counselor verifies the data. Last year, over 50 percent were admitted via this program. If an application is not auto-admitted, such as when it can't be read by computer, the assigned counselor reviews the application and makes the decision. UCR admits all applicants who meet minimum eligibility.* Transfer engineering applications go to the COE. Essays might be read at the COE only, or by both admissions staff and COE faculty. They are likely to be read only in marginal or unclear cases. *For studio art, the same process is followed for admission to the campus, but the department determines which applicants will be offered admission to the major based on a required portfolio.*

UCSB, Christian Villasenor

Transfer essays are important for borderline cases where explanation and justification of poor performance or missing preparation is looked for. Transfer essays of those who are applying to the College of L&S and who are clearly eligible receive little weight. *The essays of applicants who hold an approved transfer admission agreement are rarely read.* Personal Statements for engineering and competitive science majors may receive more weight: readers look for experience related to the field. The Faculty Admission and Enrollment Committee determines selection criteria and the weight of the criteria. For majors in the College of L&S, general admissions staff are the readers. For majors in the COE, admissions staff screen for minimum requirements and then pass on the applications to the COE where the applications are reviewed by faculty and the assistant dean.

UCSC, Michael McCawley
Occasionally, a borderline (eligibility) transfer student's personal statement might be read if a reviewer is trying to decide whether to recommend allowing the student to take a final eligibility class in the summer before enrollment, or in a case where the whole record is great except for a low GPA due to poor performance long ago. The vast majority of transfer applications are reviewed for academic achievement and eligibility alone. *Essays in most transfer applications don't come into play at all. The essays of applicants who have approved Guaranteed Admissions for Transfer Enrollment (GATE) agreements are not reviewed.* For most majors, general admissions staff review applications and make the selection decisions. Faculty and advisors in Engineering, Art, and Environmental Studies review corresponding applications and select students for admission to those majors.

UCSD, Nathan Evans
All personal statements are eventually read for clarification of academically related issues such as substitutions in major preparation or aberrations in the record. The essays come into play to keep people in the running, instead of ruling them out, in cases where the self-reported GPA is marginal for the major. *The statement is where an applicant should mention having repeated courses or gone through academic renewal.* The reviewer is then alerted to pay attention to the official calculation of the UC transferable GPA. No specific weight is given to the statement. Admission policy is guided by the Faculty Committee on Admissions. General admissions staff read applications and select for admission to the campus. Applications to impacted majors, such as many majors in the Jacobs School of Engineering, are evaluated by corresponding faculty and administrative staff. The role and weight of the personal statements vary by department. *Reviewers are assigned by community college.* A computer program tracks the flow of the applications.

Author's Note
It is important to mention that this information changes over time. There is a strong, though not constant, correlation between competition for openings and the significance of personal statements. Often greater competition inflates the role of transfer essays.

Suggestions Specific to Re-entry Students

During many years as a community college counselor, I have noticed how frequently students are sheepish at having taken time away from school. Some directly question whether they even have the right to be back. When the transfer application period comes around, some re-entry students express concern that time away from school will be perceived as an indication that they are flaky, irresponsible or indecisive.

At times, parents of future re-entry students reinforce this anxiety with the warnings they give as they try to discourage young adult children from withdrawing from college, even when the students themselves wish to do so. Years later, when these now older adult children resume their education, they are haunted by their parents' warnings. Hence, the myth of the dangers of withdrawing from college are perpetuated. Sometimes worries stem simply from the misperception that only people in their late teens and early twenties belong in college.

Many returning students use their time away from academia to pursue careers. When workers choose to leave a career, they may have doubts about being perceived as indecisive or unable to commit. Michael Dang of UC Davis shares a more positive perception, however. "[In essays,] stories of nonacademic life experience during time away from school are compelling if the presentation makes clear that to come back to school required a strong passion to change one's life."

The following prompt #1 response clearly conveys such passion.

> Numerous past experiences have led me to enjoy studying business and economics above all other coursework. As a result, I have chosen Business as my major area of study.
>
> At seventeen, I left high school and started working as an assistant at a software company in the Silicon Valley. I became a salesman after just a few weeks, and after two years, when the opportunity arose, I became the sales manager. I was relied upon for my knowledge and expertise in our software and target market. Committed to the job, I developed new ways of generating sales.
>
> In this position, I did over a quarter of a million dollars in gross profit annual sales. As a result, I made a very good income for a young man of twenty, and was grateful for the opportunity. Not only was my job financially rewarding, but it also gave me my first opportunity to learn sales, marketing, and management in a small but international business environment.
>
> By the time I reached twenty-one, I grew concerned about my lack of education, and I decided to leave the company in order to focus on school. I knew I wanted the know-how to run a business efficiently and professionally.
>
> Before starting junior college, I had never experienced teachers with such passion for the subjects they were teaching. I was able to appreciate their enthusiasm as a result of my own newly acquired interest in learning. My best role models have been my teachers and the scholars I have studied. Developing as a student has been a triumph for me.
>
> In accounting classes, I have learned the anatomy of business. I had previously thought of accounting as merely "bean counting." However, my instructor told us repeatedly that "accounting is hot stuff." He taught me the art of running a successful business as though he were Sun Tzu teaching *The Art of War*. Never before junior college had I experienced

teachers with such passion for the subjects they were teaching. No doubt my newly acquired interest in learning made me notice my teachers' enthusiasm.

In macroeconomics, I developed an interest in the theoretical factors that drive an economy. Microeconomics taught me that supply and demand is the basis of a market. My instructor gave me a new perspective on the study of finance. While recognizing the value of all academic subjects, he made it seem as though business would be the most worthwhile and interesting to study. This reconfirmed my belief I would find my place in the world in business. However, through the course of college I have broadened my academic pursuits to encompass areas such as philosophy, math and political science.

College has expanded my perspective. Beyond my hands-on work experience, college accounting and economics courses have taught me methodologies for business management.

What I like best about commerce is what it promotes: technological advances, international relations and the exchange of knowledge and resources. People from everywhere in the world long to take part in America's free enterprise system that is bolstered by an open and legal infrastructure. I have been blessed with this opportunity by being born American, and if the study of business management and financial markets will give me the skill to become a successful businessman, I embrace that opportunity. (Community College Transfer Applicant to the UC)

Not only does this applicant convincingly clarify what he did with his years between high school and community college, he persuasively explains the influence of his career on his choice of major. His discussions of what he gained from his work experiences flows naturally. The student is intelligent enough to make connections between complex concepts and understands the technicalities of his major. This essay's greatest weakness is redundancy in its midsection.

When workers are laid off, their self-esteem often takes a hit. They fear that they will be thought of as incompetent or somehow faulty. In the context of transfer, this fear is groundless. Admissions professionals understand the ups and downs of the economy and do not blame those who are disadvantaged because of it. The contributions, views, and skills of people who have worked in the non-academic world are viewed as irreplaceable during classroom discussions and in the context of university clubs, events, committees and governance. Admissions personnel, as well as faculty, fully appreciate a wide scope of perspectives in university communities.

Also great is the anxiety of some re-entry students who devoted years to homemaking. I have often heard parents worry they will not be able to adjust to an adult academic environment. Some lament, "For years I hardly ever spoke with other adults or picked up a book. The discussions I had were mostly about potty training. The books I read were about Thomas, the Train. How can I now critically analyze the works of Shakespeare or Marx?" Even when these students have spent time at the community college to re-acclimate, they are intimidated by the mystique of four-year universities.

Although it is true that transfer applicants are asked to explain gaps in their educational records, it is not the case that students are being asked to defend or justify those gaps. The explanation requested serves two purposes: to clarify for admissions reviewers that there are no college transcripts being hidden and to give applicants an opportunity to draw connections between their non-academic life experiences and their return to higher education. The explanation that is asked for is *not* indicative of accusation or judgment on the part of the university.

Of course, many returning students are not distracted by worries about whether or not they belong. They renew their participation in higher education with pride in their life choices and the experience they have gained. Their essays are more likely to acknowledge their accomplishments and contributions in a wide variety of contexts. Such essays more often address personal and professional growth as it pertains to studying at the university level. I encourage *all* re-entry students, regardless of how they spent their time away from school, to write admissions essays that acknowledge and affirm their positive traits that were revealed during time away from college.

After working for many years, one re-entry applicant spent a year traveling the world. I asked her how her re-entry status influenced her personal statement and how her statement was different from what she would have written as a high school applicant. "In high school, my essay would have been based mostly on my academic and extra-curricular but school-related activities. This essay was based much more on what I felt I could bring to the university and other students. As a re-entry student with all the experiences I've had, I have a greater appreciation that anything is possible and that being pigeonholed by other people's expectations is not a good thing. Even my class participation will likely encourage others to be open to opportunities beyond the norm."

I made sure to ask the admissions professionals about their perceptions of re-entry transfer students during interviews. The admissions administrators acknowledged the apologetic tone of many re-entry students' applications and essays. Without exception, however, these folks were emphatic in their affirmation that re-entry students, including homemakers, contribute significantly to the richness of the university community, inside the classroom and out of it. I am pleased to challenge the myth that re-entry students are not as desirable candidates for admission as are recent high school graduates. UC Riverside is one campus that admitted a 70-year-old man for the 2003-2004 academic year.

Consider the suggestion and encouragement of Marguerite Bonous-Hammarth of UC Irvine regarding homemakers.

> Take inventory of the skills you've gained and demonstrated during your time as a homemaker. Make the connections between those skills and your choice to return to college and your choice of major....There is no need to feel apologetic about having taken time off for homemaking. Often the achievement of these applicants is exceptional *because* they've been gone from school while homemaking. This can be very helpful.

UC Berkeley's Pam Burnett cautions, however,

> At the very least [re-entry students] should have coursework that demonstrates preparation for transfer to the university. If they have no other experience than homemaking, this could work against them. They have to remember that their applications are competing against others that may better demonstrate attributes relevant to success at the university. A lot will depend on how they present their experience—in their discussion, are they able to tie in some of their homemaking skills with success at the university? Did they demonstrate leadership through their role in the PTA, for instance? They should not assume that the reader will understand the challenges of homemaking. They need to describe their management of the challenges. Selective description and elaboration is important.

There are other considerations that re-entry students should take into account in writing their personal statements. Bob Giomi of UC Berkeley's College of Engineering concisely summarizes an approach recommended by admissions professionals in general. "[Re-entry students] should definitely make clear that they *are* re-entry students. The essay should reflect their thinking process regarding what brought them back to school and to engineering [or any other major] specifically." Even more significant than an explanation of why education was interrupted is a discussion of why education was resumed.

The writing skills of returning students who have not taken writing classes or written professionally for some time may be rusty enough that their ability to fully articulate about themselves may be compromised. Such students should take advantage of any number of resources to remind themselves of the basics of good writing. They can review writing manuals, take English composition courses, or request tutoring from people with a solid grounding in English, for example.

When re-entry students have early academic records that reflect poor performance, a discussion of *how* that performance changed is essential. Without some explanation of how the change happened, admissions personnel may find it difficult to trust that old patterns that compromised academic performance in the past will not return.

One issue arises because many universities do not yet fully accommodate part-time study. According to some interviewees, community college students who are enrolled part-time before transfer should convey that they understand the different level of rigor required by full-time study and that they are ready for that full-time commitment. If students are transferring to a university that operates on a quarter system from a college on a semester system, they should consider taking at least one class at a community college with a schedule similar to that of the university's. Some community college students can access courses at a university on the quarter system through cross- or concurrent-enrollment. Passing those courses demonstrates that they can handle the faster pace.

For the most part, essay discussions should relate to one's history as an adult. Re-entry students shouldn't focus a great deal on high school experiences. Mention of high school should be discussed in relation to the present or future. A diagnosis of a learning disability during high school, for instance, shouldn't merely be named, but should be talked about in such a way that the topic is seen as timely. A discussion should follow that describes how that learning disability was overcome so that success at the community college was achieved. Some childhood experiences are so monumental that they must be addressed to elicit an adequate understanding of the applicant. Such references, however, must be discussed in the context of how they pertain to the applicant's academic goals or readiness for the university.

A condensed excerpt of this UC re-entry transfer applicant's personal statement was used in the introductory chapter. The essay has some weaknesses as well as strengths, so a critique of it should be instructive.

> My husband's heart attack threw me back into the work environment. My life felt like it had been turned upside down. My husband needed surgery, we had no income from his business, no health insurance, and it had been over 25 years since I had attended secretarial school. I managed to obtain quick employment on a production line with a computer company. Getting up at 3:30 every morning for a 12 hours shift was not my idea of enjoyable. One day I spotted the president of the company in the hallway, I gathered up all my courage, stuffed my anxiety in my pocket, and walked up to him, introduced myself, and stated that I had secretarial experience and would like him to review my application. Within two weeks I had secured a position as administrative assistant to a vice president. Now, I had to prove myself. It took hard work and long hours, but I slowly gained new confidence as I became proficient in my job. I took advantage of training seminars and took evening extension courses for 2 years...I earned a certificate in marketing communications. The knowledge I gained was intellectually stimulating and gave me the confidence that I lacked. I slowly advanced to a high profile position working for the chairman of the board of the company.
>
> When my husband's health problems returned, I was forced to quit my job and take over the responsibilities in my husband's office. Again, I was thrown into a situation which I was not qualified for, but I had gained enough confidence and determination to know I could manage this challenge, too. I managed to organize projects by attacking each one individually. My biggest obstacle was learning a computerized bookkeeping program because I had no education in this area. I sought out someone to help me. Just when things were beginning to run smoothly, I was told I had an advanced state of osteoporosis. I somehow knew that this diagnosis was not correct, so I enrolled in a nutrition class at [the community college] to find out all I could about this disease. The knowledge I gained allowed me the courage to challenge the doctor's findings. Even though the doctor was adamant about the validity of his diagnosis, I persevered and discovered a mistake had indeed been made and I didn't have the disease after all. I realized how important it was for me to believe in my own intuition, take charge to find the information I need, and not be afraid to challenge the establishment.
>
> When the last of my four children left for college, I decided it was time for me to seriously pursue getting a degree so I could continue developing my career. With the support of my family, I increased my class

load at [the community college] while still working in our office. During this time I was also appointed by the [local] city council as a commissioner on the...Cultural and Preservation Commission. The combination of my courses and my position as a commissioner sparked an insatiable thirst for knowledge in the fields of Anthropology and Art History. After 10 years, I received an Associate's Degree...with a 3.89 GPA.

This essay would be easier to read if a number of the sentences were less wordy. Some of the descriptive details were superfluous because they were redundant. An example is "I gathered up all my courage, stuffed my anxiety in my pocket, and walked up to him, introduced myself, and stated that I had secretarial experience and would like him to review my application." Gathering courage and stuffing anxiety in one's pocket are images that convey an identical message. Here, walking up to someone and introducing oneself are similar enough that both phrases are not necessary. In this case, the idea of introduction is preferable because it is more active, assertive and polite. This sentence, as well as others, lacks parallel structure.

The applicant, however, is more effective in writing this essay than ineffective. This re-entry student fully accounts for her years away from school. No suspicion is raised that she may be hiding an early record. She explains her life with stories that underscore strengths that facilitate success in academia even though the stories took place outside of it. She acknowledges what she has gained from each experience. She draws connections between her responses to problems in her family and her readiness for the university. Her immediate response to the heart attack, for instance, indicates a strong sense of responsibility and teamwork. When I picture her participating in group assignments for class, I picture her as an active group member. Resourcefulness is illustrated by her stories of learning the computerized bookkeeping program and studying nutrition in order to be an informed participant in her own medical treatment. I don't doubt that she would ultimately find whatever she might be looking for within the UC library system or beyond it. The role she took in reaction to being misdiagnosed offers further evidence that this woman possesses solid critical thinking skills. She gives multiple examples, such as the completion of a certificate in marketing communication and an associate's degree, of following through on commitments, despite daunting life challenges. The last paragraph identifies the applicant as a multi-tasker and participant in her community. It is likely that she will participate in the university community, as well.

Although she recognizes significant hardships in her life, she focuses on her *responses* to them so that she avoids any tone of self-pity. Her mention of her high GPA is in context so she is not merely repeating information found elsewhere in the application, but adding on to it. As a whole, the essay imparts to us the impression that the writer is dedicated enough to reach any goal she sets for herself, no matter how long it takes to do so. Instead of sounding worried about her age and re-entry status, she takes advantage of her life experience to make it easy for us to believe in her potential for success at the university.

English as a Second Language (ESL), Writing Technicalities, and Review

This section groups together information about ESL, grammar, and composition. The chart that follows shortly organizes distinct views on these topics by campus.

Cohesive Essay or Simple Answer

Some admissions professionals strongly believe that the responses to personal statement questions should be treated as assigned essays for class, with corresponding attention to grammar, structure, and flow of content. Others are firm in the opinion that the responses should be treated as answers to questions and nothing more. Some make a point to avoid using the word "essay" when discussing the personal statement because it implies something more technically sophisticated than a straightforward answer to a straightforward question. For some readers, presentation adds to the impression left by the content of a response; for others, content is the *only* consideration taken into account.

Review

Admissions staff are similarly divided on the importance, morality, and purpose of having other people proofread essays. Some admissions administrators believe that essays should only be proofread for items of grammar. Others believe it is appropriate for informal reviewers to check that an adequate sense of the applicant's personality is being conveyed. Some professionals indicate that strangers make better reviewers because they don't have a preconceived notion of the applicant and because some applicants omit private but important information when someone close to them may read their essays. Other professionals, in contrast, say that personal friends and family make the best reviewers because they notice if the students have left out something important about themselves or their experiences.

Different people will notice and pay attention to different aspects of a written work as they review. An applicant to a graduate program in public policy asked a colleague and me to review her statement of intent. I read her essay, making a few comments in the margins to suggest more detail, and passed the statement on to my coworker. My coworker noticed something I had missed: in the first line of the essay, the student had left out the letter "l" from the word "public." Such an error is unlikely to make the difference between getting into a program or not—but it is an error most of us would not want part of our official documents!

English as a Second Lanuguage (ESL)

J. Jesus Lopez Zavala, another transfer graduate of the UC system, describes some of the concerns he had as an ESL applicant who immigrated from Mexico,

> I like writing so I enjoyed the challenge of writing the application essay. But one thing that made it difficult was writing in English, because I am a native Spanish-speaker. Also, I didn't know if it would work against me if I sounded like an immigrant in the way I wrote. I struggled with how to say what I wanted to say and overcome possible cultural barriers. Some

concepts are meaningful for the Mexican Latino culture but have less significance or a different meaning for people of some other cultures. The idea of adult children living with their parents, for example, is often perceived of differently between different cultures... I knew that I would make mistakes in grammar and that I would get writing help. I wondered if that was cheating.

Transfer students should know that readers are usually trained regarding cultural and language patterns likely to arise in personal statements. With experience, readers further develop awareness through noticing recurring themes and language errors in the essays written by applicants of various cultures.

I present admissions professionals' comments in this chart because the range of opinions is so great. It is important to note that admissions administrators acknowledge that readers, *even at the same campus*, may differ on these points.

Chart 1: Writing (Paraphrased Responses)

Question	UCB, Pam Burnett	UCB, COE, Bob Giomi	UCD, Michael Dang	UCI, Marguerite Bonous-Hammarth, Ph.D.	UCLA, Lena Brown
How important is it for the writing to be grammatically correct?	We're not reading the essays as though we're English teachers. The content is primary, but competition is fierce so any edge is good.	Show you care by at least using the spell check and grammar check programs on your computer.	We place no emphasis on this, but good writing and coherent elegance can't help but be a plus.	Very important. The responses have to be well written so the important information can be easily extracted.	This is more important for transfer students. At the least, computerized spelling and grammar checks should be used.
Are the introductory and concluding sentences and paragraphs significant in the personal statement?	We're looking for content only.	There is value in engaging the reader right away. Conclusions should tie in the content with applicant goals.	Make the essays as easy to read as possible. The real question is, "Is the content there?"	The flow is important.	No. Don't get stuck on syntax.
Some ESL students who lack fluency in English express concern that they are at a disadvantage. What is your feedback?	We're looking for content only.	Keep sentences simple. This can still get the point across.	Is the writing clear enough to convey the necessary information? We're not focused on grammar. Longer words are not necessarily impressive—don't rely too much on the thesaurus!	It's often easier for ESL students to write in the first person.	For many, the only issue here is confidence. The small errors typical of ESL students are overlooked.

Question	UCB, Pam Burnett	UCB, COE, Bob Giomi	UCD, Michael Dang	UCI, Marguerite Bonous-Hammarth, Ph.D.	UCLA, Lena Brown
What is your opinion about having a number of people review applicants' statements before submission?	This is recommended. Reviewers should identify where more descriptive details are needed. All the words should be the applicants'.	Good idea. Others' perspectives are a good way to keep the bigger picture in mind.	Reviewers should be friends who know you and who can evaluate if you are accurately conveying a sense of yourself. They should be good friends who have the ability to be honest with you. They shouldn't be reviewing so much for grammar.	There should be at least one review for grammar and another for the quality of the writing.	Don't ask family or friends for a review if there's something in the personal statement you might not want them to see. Have reviewers assess if the responses make sense and accurately reflect who you are.

Chart 1: Writing (continued)

Question	UCM, ER, SF, LJ	UCR, LaRae Lundgren	UCSB, Christian Villasenor	UCSC, Michael McCawley	UCSD, Nathan Evans
How important is it for the writing to be grammatically correct?	Important. This reflects maturity, responsibility, and resourcefulness.	There's no penalty given for mistakes, but presentation makes a difference. Treat this like an English class assignment. Do at least 2 to 3 drafts.	We don't penalize students for errors, but strong writing is a plus for applicants who are on the edge of an offer of admission. Strong writing demonstrates a readiness for university level work.	Not very important. Writing that is too perfect can raise questions of authenticity—responses must be written by the applicant.	We are only taking into account the content. The writing only needs to be strong enough to convey the content clearly.
Are the introductory and concluding sentences and paragraphs significant in the personal statement?	In the shorter responses, especially, there isn't room for this. Don't think of these responses as essays, but as answers. Content is primary.	Presentation to and orientation of the reader is important. This should be treated like an assignment for a class.	No. What is being looked for is specific information and explanation. College academic performance is what counts most.	Think of this task more as one of answering questions rather than writing an essay.	Just convey the elicited information.

Question	UCM, ER, SF, LJ	UCR, LaRae Lundgren	UCSB, Christian Villasenor	UCSC, Michael McCawley	UCSD, Nathan Evans
Some ESL students who lack fluency in English express concern that they are at a disadvantage. What is your feedback?	The content is most important. University readers recognize and overlook common ESL errors. Ask for proofreading help.	Ask someone proficient in English for assistance in proofreading. Use a grammar and spell check program.	Make clear you are an ESL student. The grades in the English composition classes are what count. Grammar in the essay is not as important.	The writing level can be important in cases where the applicant's TOEFL scores or Engl. Composition class grades do not make them clearly eligible.	Just convey the elicited information.
What is your opinion about having a number of people review applicants' statements before submission?		One reviewer may be enough if s/he is knowledgeable about English. Keep your authentic voice.	Don't have too many reviewers. Get someone who is a stranger to see if you adequately communicate a sense of who you are. Have someone else review for grammar. Too many reviewers can lead to contradictory suggestions.	Some review for proofreading is fine, but the essay should reflect the student's voice and writing level and be written by the applicant alone.	Reviewers should only make sure that the answers speak to the prompts. If the content is private in nature, a review by someone else is not necessary.

Example of Problematic Writing Quality

Of the essays included in this guide, the quality of writing in the following is the most problematic.

My intended major at UC_ is Sociology. I hope to one day use my bachelors degree to obtain a Masters in Social Work. My interest in the field of Sociology developed as a young boy. Growing up as the middle child of five I was able to observe several different age groups and how they interacted with each other. I am only a few years apart from all my siblings giving me the chance to have peer conversations with them during my childhood and on into my adult life. The intimacy of these relationships helped train me to automatically lend an ear to a friend or acquaintance in need. At the beginning of my second year at the community college I joined the honor society Alpha Gamma Sigma. A.G.S. is well known as an academic honor society however a major component to one,s membership in the club is community service. Soon after joining I found out about a volunteer opportunity to tutor high school kids at _____ school located on the community college campus. _____ is an alternative school for students who do not adapt well in a regular high school environment. At _____ I worked one-on-one with kids who needed special attention by assisting them with assignments and projects. I also took full advantage of the chance to observe student interactions whenever I could. The experience at ____ was great; soon after working there I knew I wanted to be a teacher one day. For now the experience helped me better realize my true objective of working with the kids outside the classroom. In the last six months I have made leaps and bounds in my pursuit of working with teenagers in that very format. Soon after my girlfriend,s father passed away (See Question 3) during the spring of 2003 I re-assessed my life and felt I needed to more actively pursue my goals. Initally I became a volunteer at the _____ Teen Center mentoring teenagers in an open group forum. Now every Friday I work their doing my best to provide a fun, safe and open environment for all to enjoy. At the Teen Center I have helped tackle difficult youth issues, organize dances and concerts in order to promote youth safety. My volunteer experience helped open the door to my current employment at a group home. With some persistence I convinced the administrator of the group home that I was ready and able to work as a counselor in his facility. I knew I was ready because my drive to get involved with my willingness to work hard was in high gear. The group home is called the ___ House and there I help provide care for six boys. Like a parent I am responsible for each boys mental and physical being, which in-tails a great many things. Some of the aspects I focus on most are schoolwork, exercise, diet, hygiene, respect, responsibility and communication. This means at my job I am a tutor, homemaker, chauffeur, mentor, mediator, teacher and friend.

Since I began working with the boys I have learned a lot. This job has helped out my ability to communicate and be organized as well as strengthened my patience. Without some of these skills I could not command the boys trust the way I do and I could not be the good role model for them that I am. My involvement at the ____House, Teen Center, and alternative school has really helped fuel and give substance to my desire of working with young adults. This type of active fieldwork has facilitated my confidence in myself professionally as well as academically.

When an error is a lone aberration, readers can more comfortably dismiss it as an oversight in an otherwise well-written piece. In this essay, punctuation, especially commas and apostrophes, is misused and absent throughout the essay. The omission recurs so regularly that it indicates a lack of knowledge of the rules of punctuation. Paragraph breaks would make the essay easier to follow. A number of sentences are too lengthy and fall short on parallel construction and are, therefore, hard to follow. The author probably means "entails" where he has written "in-tails." This may be an example of trying to use words that are not part of one's regular vocabulary, or perhaps it is simply a spelling error. Either way, it is distracting and fails to impress.

This student's concrete work experience makes him seem an appropriate candidate more than does his discussion of family intimacy. If the author believes it is important to talk about his experiences in his family, perhaps that talk should appear later in the essay instead of early on. Applicants should put the most relevant and impressive information first. A chronological structure is not always the best way to highlight what is most important.

Phrases such as "tackle difficult youth issues" are vague. Does the writer mean he talked over difficult personal problems with the teens or that he developed intervention programs to address community problems involving youth, or what?

The content of the essay does deliver some significant positive impressions. The writer lets us know that his career goals of teaching and social work have been confirmed by actual related experience. He informs us that he has further tested his passion for helping teens by working with them in a variety of roles and contexts. In general, we are given solid descriptions of tasks completed and skills developed. These skills include organization, communication, and mediation, all of which can be useful in a university community. In addition, we learn that this applicant has initiative and persistence—both demonstrated by his pursuit and acquisition of a position that entails a great deal of responsibility.

I fear that weaknesses in the writing are so consistent that they mask or distract from this student's strengths, many of which are admirable and relevant.

General Writing Suggestions

Following is a list that summarizes additional writing suggestions.
- Don't repeat without expanding upon points made elsewhere in the application
- Make each sentence count
- Don't write a comprehensive autobiography unless you are asked for one
- Depth and substance are usually more persuasive than quantity

- Don't emphasize creativity, originality, or humor if doing so is at the expense of answering the question and communicating important information about yourself
- Strike a balance between a personal and formal tone
- Be direct
- Don't over-generalize or assume readers will agree with you
- Proofread
- Don't convey a tone of apology or desperation
- Don't preach or lecture
- Say everything you need to say to answer the question and paint a picture, but do it with as few words as possible
- No put-downs
- Highlight strengths and preparedness
- Follow the instructions
- Use active and descriptive words, rather than passive and general words

"Help" is a generic word that is often used ineffectively in essays. Applicants frequently discuss wanting to help people, for instance. In this context, "to help" might mean to *heal, teach, empower, feed or organize*. The writer might intend to *build shelters, serve as an advocate or translate for people*. Although this list of possibilities is not complete, it hopefully conveys the difference between general words such as "help" and active and descriptive ones. Word choice influences how well or poorly readers understand applicants. Many resume guides provide lists of active verbs and adjectives.

Campus-specific Discussion in Essay Content

Many students are under the impression that they should specify in their statements why they want to attend their first choice campuses. Yet most students, who wisely apply to more than one campus, fear that emphasizing an affinity for one campus will alienate or offend admissions representatives at others.

Michael Dang of UC Davis is the only UC interviewee who unequivocally encouraged applicants to explain their choice of the Davis campus. He explained that UCD is unable to admit all qualified applicants to their preferred majors. The explanation of a preference for Davis is useful in cases in which applicants to competitive majors are on the edge of an offer of admissions.

Bob Giomi of UCB's College of Engineering, Pam Burnett of UCB, and Lena Brown of UCLA discouraged applicants from discussing their choice of campus and did not mention any exceptional situations. Lena Brown, however, acknowledged that some transfer applicants' lives are entrenched in the LA area and that this should be explained in the personal statement.

Other admissions professionals also discouraged talk of campus preference. They indicated that an applicant should explain the choice of campus only when that campus is the *sole* UC campus to which the student is applying. It is not recommended that students apply to only one campus, but some students do limit themselves to a single choice.

An applicant who does discuss the reasons for the choice of campus should connect the explanation with one of the prompts. Explanations of the choice of campus should identify reasons that are unique to the campus and the applicant. In most cases, the preference for one campus should reflect that the applicant has conducted in-depth research of the campus and major. Discussion of campus appeal should refer only to attributes of substance. Mention of the beauty of the area or reputation of the campus is trite and general. It adds no new information and is, consequently, a waste of precious word allotments. A desire to study or research under a specific faculty member with a rare specialization that coincides with the applicant's academic interests, on the other hand, is an example of a reason that is substantive. Applicants should be careful with even this kind of explanation, though, because mere name-dropping is transparent.

Discussions of first choice campus should focus on what the choice reveals about the applicants. Applicants may choose to discuss experiences that demonstrate personal qualities that fit in with a specific campus community. Or applicants may need to reveal private medical information about themselves, a parent, or a child by way of explaining the need to pursue academic goals in a specific region.

Suggestions for Addressing Trauma and Hardship

One transfer student admitted to the UC system voiced doubts shared by many applicants as they choose between discussing and not discussing highly personal life challenges: "I worried about whether or not to mention my divorce. I wondered if divorce is too personal to talk about in the personal statement. Is it appropriate? Would they [the readers] think I was being manipulative and trying to get them to feel sorry for me so they would select me? Eventually, I decided to mention the sudden end of my marriage because it was the curve ball that explains why I'm coming back to school at this time." This applicant recognized the relevance of this incident to her educational history and, consequently, saw the propriety of mentioning it.

A number of personal statements already examined have identified traumas or hardships confronted by the applicants. The stories of financial hardship (in the section on prompt #3) and a spouse's heart attack (in the section on suggestions for re-entry students) are examples. This next section expands upon the discussion of when and how best to include such accounts.

Lena Brown of UC Los Angeles assures transfer applicants, "You *don't* have to have a 'woe is me' story to write a strong personal statement and be selected. On the other hand, *everyone* has faced a challenge of some kind, especially transfer students." The key to deciding whether or not to talk about a challenge depends on whether or not the applicant can put into words how the challenge has influenced academically-related choices, opportunities, or performance. UC Riverside's LaRae Lundgren reiterates, "Include this [discussion of hardship] only if it is part of an answer to a prompt." Even then, she adds, "Pay attention to how you discuss it. Focus on what you've learned from it, what it's driven you to do, how it has shaped who you are and influenced your goals and beliefs. Don't dwell on the trauma itself."

Admissions professionals agree that the more detailed discussion should be about the applicants' *responses* to hardships, not the hardships themselves. University of Southern California's Kirk Brennan articulates a common perspective:

> If the trauma has influenced performance and there's been a rebound and the student is now performing well, we need an adequate description of the facts and then a focus on how the challenge was overcome. If there's

no discussion of the rebound, the mention of the trauma...seems pointless. We want to know that the applicants can *now* handle the many challenges of the large and competitive...[university] campus. Overcoming a variety of challenges and persistence are important skills at the university level.

UC Santa Barbara's Christian Villasenor gives an example. One year, UCSB received applications from two students who mentioned having suffered from eating disorders. For a while, the academic performance of both applicants was compromised. Later, the performance of both improved. One applicant mentioned the illness perfunctorily. The message she conveyed was that she had been sick and wasn't able to succeed academically for a time, but that she got over it and then earned good grades again. This is acceptable. However, the other applicant described studying about the disease to understand it better, getting counseling, and then talking with other sufferers to help them recover. Most readers would find it easier to trust that the eating disorder of the second student will not recur. Furthermore, the second applicant used her discussion of the hardship to inform readers of her intellectual curiosity, resourcefulness, self-awareness, and concern for others.

A focus on *overcoming* hardship not only emphasizes an applicant's strengths, it also circumvents the risk of appearing to be asking for admission based on pity. One of the interviewees sees the waste of an opportunity in a typically ineffective approach that looks like, "I have a learning disability. Please make an exception for me," without any further elaboration of how the applicant has overcome the hardship to achieve academically. In this type of situation, complete explanations of how applicants have approached coping with the learning disabilities, or other challenges, are significantly more helpful. Especially when applicants are requesting the waiver of an admission requirement, professionals want to know if the applicants have taken the initiative to seek out resources to help themselves. Readers want to know that applicants challenged by learning disabilities, for example, have explored all appropriate alternatives before asking for admission based on exception. Only discussions of the *management* of hardships reveal such information.

Most admissions professionals acknowledge that some applicants find it difficult to discuss private hardships in their personal statements. A few UC interviewees mentioned that it is acceptable for transfer students to refrain from sharing material that feels too personal. Applicants may be admitted without having to expose sensitive and private aspects of their histories. If they are not, they are encouraged to include their private stories in letters of appeal. The new supplemental information will be taken into account and might facilitate late offers of admission.

The following is an excerpt of a personal statement that includes discussion of overcoming hardship:

> In the spring of 2000, I took a semester off after I had gotten out of a rehabilitation program. I needed time to focus on my health, recovery, and myself. Throughout my life, I have perpetuated guilt, shame, fear, and self-hatred. I was continuing a cycle of violence against self that I learned at an early age. I had reached a point where I could no longer afford these beliefs and since then, I have been on a path of growth and

acceptance. I am now on a path for which I have a future. Today I am learning how to face my fears and show up for my life no matter what. Every day I work for positive transformation. I am learning how to accept myself and love myself for being exactly who I am. In December, I will have four years clean and sober while maintaining a GPA of 3.9 since returning to school. In addition to attending community college almost full time and 30 hours of work a week, I am a member of the Honor Society and I am of service in recovery. (Community College Transfer Student Admitted to the UC)

Even though the wordiness of this excerpt requires us to work to extract information, the excerpt does reveal an impressive response to addiction. This student withstood the ordeal of a rehabilitation program, took time to pursue recovery activities, and has maintained sobriety for four years. She has stayed sober despite the stress of balancing work and school well enough to achieve outstanding academic success. She is capable of introspection and is insightful. The writer does not need to discuss when the addiction started, how long she was using, or the object of her addiction. She doesn't even need to discuss what triggered her to participate in a rehabilitative program. The details here are barely about the addiction she battles; instead, they are about her understanding and recovery. The discussion would be stronger with a little more detail about the specifics of her voluntary recovery activities and less detail regarding personal insights about her psyche and past.

At one time, the UC constructed a personal statement topic with the use of the word "hardship." Unfortunately, the public interpreted this as an implication that students who wrote about hardships would be more likely to be admitted. This was not, and is not, the case. Although the UC has changed the wording of the prompts, the myth that a dramatic story increases one's chances of admission persists. Applicants should realize that made-up or exaggerated stories of hardship are highly transparent, especially when compared to authentic accounts. Such stories do not succeed in convincing readers.

Discussions of Ethnicity and Other Aspects of Identity That Have Been Targets of Discrimination

"When Juliana was asked to check a box identifying her race or ethnicity on some official form, she, like an increasing number of Americans, felt justified in marking more than one. In fact, she checked three. 'When I check one box,' Juliana explained, ' I feel like I'm denying part of myself"(Jacques Steinberg, The Gatekeepers: Inside the Admissions Process of a Premier College [New York: Penguin, 2002] 28).

Checking such boxes to identify race or ethnicity is not the only uncomfortable task of this kind for many applicants. Many transfer students struggle with deciding whether or not to discuss, in their personal statements, the ethnicity, race, sexual orientation or culture with which they identify. Some fear that their motives for such discussions will be misunderstood. Some applicants fear they will be admitted to serve only as token representatives or that they will be denied admission because of bigotry. Others fear the perception that they are trying to evoke sympathy for being associated with a group underrepresented in higher education. As one applicant explained,

> I didn't feel comfortable discussing being someone who is racially mixed because if I talked about my ethnicity, I worried that my application would be thrown out due to a hypersensitivity against affirmative action principles. And I didn't want anyone to think I was using my ethnic background to get *into* school either. (Community College Transfer Admit to the UC).

Ultimately, some applicants feel too uncomfortable and decide not to raise the issue of ethnicity, race, or culture. Another transfer applicant commented,

> I didn't know if it was a good thing to present myself as a Japanese-American lesbian. If I talked about it, would I be seen as trying to play a sympathy card? I was uncertain about its relevance. Ultimately, I decided I wanted to be looked at for my performance alone, so I left out this discussion. (Community College Transfer Admit to the UC)

In contrast, other applicants decide that the issue is too important and relevant to their stories to leave out. Some sample essay excerpts in the sections on responding to prompts #2 and #3, and on controversial topics and avoiding boasting, are examples that demonstrate appropriate and effective reference to ethnicity, culture and other aspects of identity that have been targets of discrimination historically.

The UC asserts that applicants need not fear bigotry in the selection process and that readers are thoroughly and carefully trained to avoid it.

The recommended approach to *how* to discuss such issues stresses how the issue is a relevant part of a response to a prompt. Discussion of identity should clarify educational choices, enhance understanding of educational history (including the overcoming of barriers), or explain potential to contribute. Although issues of identity are always relevant in applicants' lives, the challenge in the personal statement is to spell out, on paper, that relevance. Applicants should not assume that readers understand the relevance without having it explained to them. Free-floating mention of how one identifies oneself serves little or no purpose in the selection process. There is no "right" or "wrong" answer as to whether or not to discuss these issues—the bottom line is that each applicant must make his/her own decision because it these considerations are so very personal in nature.

A Lack of Out-of-Classroom Experience

The topic of a lack of out-of-classroom experience evoked a wide variety of responses on the part of admission administrators. The most basic consideration is to remember that all applicant essay content should address a prompt.

Community college transfer applicants should feel comforted that discussion of out-of-classroom experience is not essential in all personal statements. As Michael Dang of UC Davis acknowledges,

> Some students haven't had the chance to pursue much out-of-classroom experience due to family obligations, etc. Or maybe it's not culturally acceptable to spend time gaining a lot of out-of-classroom and out-of-

home experience. This is not necessarily a disadvantage. We know that community college students often don't have the luxury to gain this kind of experience. This will not be held against them.

Lena Brown of UC Los Angeles adds, "If they [transfer applicants] have been working and/or raising a family while attending school, the university is not putting weight on other extracurricular activities. All of that is enough!"

Other suggestions pertained to persuasive elaboration on in-classroom experience. Exploration of what was gained from in-class projects and influential lectures, assignments, or professors can leave a positive impression. Students who haven't had the opportunity to search out internships, for example, can nevertheless capitalize upon classroom experiences. The engineering-related excerpt, included in the section on responses to prompt #1, offers an impressive account of the influence of an assignment for class.

Controversial Topics

I once read a personal statement by an aspiring Environmental Studies major. In it, the student attempted to teach readers his theories about current challenges to the environment. While doing so, he called the owners of the lumber industry "evil" and explicitly blamed them for all modern day environmental problems. Although the applicant had been asked to write about himself, the tone of his essay was one of an assigned paper because he wrote about an issue instead. Not only did this student fail to follow instructions, he discussed a controversial view in a dogmatic manner without including any basis for his opinions. The personal statement is not the right place to try to educate readers about issues. If opinions about issues are presented, they should be supported substantively. The potentially controversial nature of the topic of environmental protection was *not* the problem; the uninformed, adversarial, and overbearing manner in which it was presented was. An even greater problem was that the content of the essay did not respond in any way to the prompt about which the applicant should have written.

Given that "readers are 'normed' *not* to insert their own values into the evaluation process" (Pam Burnett, UC Berkeley), applicants need not worry about taboo subjects. However, applicants should bear in mind that the university is interested in *how* they think, not *what* they think. Any discussion that refers to potentially controversial themes should be less about the issues and more about the applicants. Again, it is imperative that any topic be relevant to the given prompt. Christian Villasenor of UC Santa Barbara suggests,

> The way [applicants] discuss these [potentially controversial] themes should indicate an understanding that, at the university, there are other views and that they [applicants] either know how or are open to learning how to deal with other views. Part of the university experience is to delve into issues, find a voice, participate in opportunities for activism, etc. So substantive opinions are accepted and acceptable. The exceptions would be examples that defy common sense and good interpersonal skills. Claims of being a terrorist or desire to commit violence would be a very

bad idea. Also, racist views would not work because campuses have policies of being racially inclusive.

Bob Giomi of UC Berkeley's College of Engineering instructs, "Either avoid controversy entirely or acknowledge the legitimacy of other views....Be humble; don't ram [your view] down the readers' throats or act like it is the only right view."

On the other hand, one admissions professional would *not* discourage dogmatic applicants from presenting one-sided discussions in their personal statements because the university wants to gain realistic and honest impressions of applicants. Also, even readers at the same campus respond differently to the same personal statement content, so trying to second-guess campus reaction is a waste of time in all but extreme cases.

UC Merced's Encarnacion Ruiz identifies discussions of potentially sensitive subjects as opportunities for positive essay content:

> [Applicants should] focus on how they are actively engaged in the issue. What have they done with their viewpoint? Did they exhibit leadership in relation to it, for example…? If they are discussing having been incarcerated, they need to discuss what they have done during that time. Did they conduct research, for instance?

The following excerpt refers to work experience regarding the theme of sexual orientation, a topic about which our society is divided. The discussion should not be problematic for admissions officers because it maintains focus on the applicant and on experience relevant to the choice of a major in Movements, Institutions, Policy, and Legal Studies. The essay never becomes dogmatic in tone. Indeed, it accomplishes what Ruiz suggests it should: it shows what the writer has "done with" the personal position presented and convincingly demonstrates qualities such as leadership, initiative, and commitment. It underscores organizational, public speaking, and interpersonal skills, as well.

> I am naturally acclimated to this field of study. When I was 16 2 friends of mine and I founded the Rainbow Alliance at ____ High School. The Rainbow Alliance was [the high school's] first Gay/Straight Alliance. During that same time, I was a bisexual speaker for Triangle Speakers. Triangle Speakers organizes panels of homosexual persons and their loved ones to speak in organizations and at schools dispelling myths and breaking down barriers of ignorance and prejudice. I was also involved with Q + A, a peer HIV/AIDS education and awareness program supported by the ____ County Aids Project.
>
> In addition to my work with peers and my community, I have also volunteered for Assembly member ____ in his [home] county office and I participated in Youth Lobby Day in Sacramento for 3 years. On Youth Day a number of young people from all over California came together at the Capitol to lobby for queer youth rights. During my third year, I was a Youth Lobby Day Leader and took students from southern California to

meet with their representatives. (Community College Transfer Student Admitted to the UC)

This impressive review of accomplishments is presented in the context of the goal of working in the field of policy and social change. An even stronger response would have explicitly spelled out elements of the match between these experiences and the chosen academic field. In addition, this student wasted an opportunity to explain what was gained from these experiences. Such changes would have helped the excerpt read less like a list. However, there is no weakness here that is due to the presentation of the potentially controversial theme of sexual orientation itself.

Writing About Talents and Accomplishments Without Boasting

The view of Kirk Brennan of Southern California University is representative of the position of UC admissions professionals, too: "It's more effective if the essay helps admissions folks understand the *importance* of the achievement or talent in the applicant's life. [Applicants] should demonstrate intention and self-awareness—have they *thought* about these activities and how they are part of who the applicants are? How have these experiences changed the applicants?" Identifying what one has learned from an experience guards against a tone of superiority. Focusing greater discussion on one or two items adds to a reader's sense of the applicant more than does a list of many items. Describing experiences instead of labeling one's own gifts and exceptional achievements maintains a sense of humility as does explaining why the experience was initially pursued. The overall message conveyed by a discussion of strengths and accomplishments should not be, "Now do you see how great I am?" Rather it should be, "Now do you better understand who I am and what motivates me?"

A number of admissions administrators were eager to point out that for many transfer students, given their life circumstances, succeeding academically is achievement enough.

The following excerpt describes achievement instead of simply labeling it. The applicant also addresses what he has gained from his experiences.

> I've taken every political science class offered at my community college. I didn't want to spend my last semester without any political science classes so I lobbied the department to run a "Current Issues in International Relations" class which will be part of the curriculum next semester. I'm currently working with my professor to develop the course syllabus. I've had to research and analyze what will be the emergent issues in the world over the next twenty years by critically looking at the news and understanding what issues underlie the stories being reported. I've had to learn how to strike a balance between the amount of information out there and what can realistically be covered in one semester. Developing this course has taught me how to take my personal bias out of the issues and present them fairly so that the course material would be accessible to all students (Community College Transfer Applicant to the UC).

This student does a fine job of describing his achievements without boasting.

It is important to mention those applicants whose challenge is to acknowledge their accomplishments at all. Unfortunately, applicants whose cultures discourage such self-praise are likely disadvantaged by this in the writing of their UC personal statements. Such applicants, as well as those with low self-esteem, might consider consulting with a college counselor to find a way to accomplish what is required by the personal statement component of the UC application without compromising their own values or writing content that feels false to the students themselves.

The Myth of Standing Out

According to UC admissions administrators, one of the most persistent and annoying myths regarding the personal statement is that its most important objective is to grab the reader's attention and make the applicant unforgettably stand out from all other applicants. The truth is that the most important objective of the essay is to convey important information about the applicant through responses to the specified prompts. This is *more* important than standing out as a memorable character. Although it is possible to catch the reader's attention as a unique applicant *and* answer the questions, it is difficult to achieve this balance via the use of gimmicks, jokes, or quirkiness. Typically, the use of such devices in essay-writing distracts from or replaces information of substance. Although even applicants who are funny or odd should strive to convey an authentic voice, they benefit from avoiding extremes in their presentation.

One of the most memorable essays I have read was written in the format of a series of "blonde jokes." Each blonde joke was followed by commentary that explained how the applicant was similar or dissimilar to the relevant stereotype to which the joke alluded. This personal statement was memorable for the wrong reasons. Everything that I learned about the student was superficial. The essay format left many holes in my understanding of the writer. I was left with an impression of immaturity, poor judgment, and desperation. The applicant would have been far better served by writing a straightforward and routine essay that thoughtfully and thoroughly spoke to all the prompts, even if today *I* no longer remembered her.

Another personal statement attempted to grab the reader's attention by confessing all the ways the applicant was *not* exceptional. The approach was old by the third sentence and I was still waiting to learn anything that was true of the applicant. I was impatient to reach the heart of the essay but got bored before I did. Admissions readers claim that when applicants attempt an overly creative approach, their essays often evoke reactions opposite from those they are seeking.

There is no rigid rule about creativity, however. Applicants who can make important information easily accessible to readers while also applying creativity should feel free to do so. The bottom line is that students should not emphasize creativity, originality, or humor *if it is at the expense of* thoroughly providing the requested information.

Other Myths and Rumors Reported by UC Admission Professionals

Myth #1: <u>Perfection is required.</u>

In fact, an essay that is too slick and refined may raise the question of authenticity. This will give the essay less weight. Random checks on claims made in essays are occasionally performed.

Myth #2: <u>Stories of hardship, drama, trauma, and tragedy make the difference between an impressive personal statement and one that is ignored.</u>

Myth #3: <u>Longer is better.</u>

Myth #4: <u>You don't have to include the personal statement in the application.</u>

Some campuses categorize applications without personal statements incomplete and, therefore, do not consider them. Applicants cannot anticipate with certainty whether or not their statements will be read.

Myth #5: <u>Strong personal statements can be produced in one sitting.</u>

Effective essays require that the prompts and personal ideas are mulled over well in advance of the actual writing. Time should be allotted for later proofreading and review as well.

Myth #6: <u>Big quotes and big words are impressive.</u>

If the applicant doesn't usually communicate this way, the lack of sincerity will be obvious. Worse, it may leave an impression of immaturity and poor judgment.

Myth #7: <u>The personal statement is usually the most important deciding factor regarding an offer of transfer admission.</u>

For transfer students who meet eligibility requirements, GPA and lower division major coursework are more important.

Myth #8: All campuses use the personal statements in the same way.

Myth #9: UC admissions readers are looking for something unstated.

Rationales are now included for each prompt in the application. There is no hidden agenda. Applicants who try to second-guess what the readers "want to see", are wasting time and energy. Given that each campus is different in its use of the essay and that even readers at the same campus may walk away with different impressions of the same essay, second-guessing is pointless. It is appropriate and important that applicants make their own decisions in the writing of their essays, even if doing so is, at times, uncomfortable.

Admission by Exception and Letters of Appeal

Admission by exception is *extremely* rare. *Admission by exception* refers to extraordinary instances in which applicants are accepted even though they lack a minimum requirement for admission. Occasionally, the explanation for the incomplete set of minimum requirements is sufficiently compelling as to convince admissions administrators that the applicant can excel at the university. Even more rare are situations in which the applicant possesses a talent or has mastered an achievement so phenomenal that to add this person to the university community is worth waiving an admissions requirement. Explanations of such exceptional circumstances are provided in the content of personal statement essays. Typically, the admissions counselors who initially review such applications pass them up to administrators who make the final decisions.

Admission by appeal occurs, albeit infrequently, after an applicant has been denied admission, even with minimum requirements met. The applicant writes a letter of appeal that adds new information not previously included in the application. The letter explains exceptional circumstances that may have lowered academic performance or quantitative measures to a level not representative of the applicant's potential. Occasionally, the letter describes life circumstances that are adequately compelling to persuade admissions administrators that their campus is indeed the *only* one that is feasible for that applicant's enrollment. Often this kind of information would have been appropriate for the personal statement essays, but was either too private in nature to include unless necessary or not timely at the moment of application. Acceptable reasons for admission by appeal differ by campus and term. An actual example is a transfer student who was initially denied admission based on senior status. This student sufficiently explained that most of the excess units were earned a long time earlier in a major unrelated to the current specified major. Another example is a transfer student who is the primary caretaker of his spouse who was recently diagnosed with cancer and whose medical treatment is limited to the region of one specific campus. As with admission by exception, admission by appeal is usually determined by admissions administrators.

Discussion of Membership in Student Programs

California Community Colleges excel at offering services and programs to assist students in achieving their academic and employment goals. Programs often depend on impermanent funding and, consequently, appear and disappear continually. Some are college-specific and many similar programs have different names at different colleges. Some of the current longstanding programs found at many colleges today include but are not limited to programs such as:

- Disabled Student Services (DSS)
- Educational Opportunities Programs and Services (EOP&S)
- Math Engineering and Science Achievement (MESA)
- The Puente Project
- Re-entry Student Services

Merely name-dropping regarding program participation is a waste of a chance to highlight impressive characteristics. Instead, applicants who choose to mention such programs should do so in the context of discussing how they sought out unique opportunities facilitated by the programs, mastered or demonstrated a skill or achievement via participation, or otherwise benefited. This approach is analogous to exploration of participation in campus clubs or activities; however, most of the *programs* specifically seek to assist students in constructively facing hardships or challenges to college success. Program participants often draw upon this distinction in their personal statement essays.

Personal statement content should be less about the manner in which the applicant meets program eligibility requirements and more about qualities relevant to academic success revealed by the unique nature of individual participation in those programs. An applicant with a psychological disability, for instance, need not write at length about the nature of the disability and its development, but can focus the larger part of the discussion on how s/he took advantage of the offerings of Disabled Student Services to stay on task enough to ultimately overcome a poor early college academic record. It is important to remember that an exploration of the applicants' own participation should dominate any discussions of program offerings and benefits.

Other Sample Essays

I'm including other sample personal statements simply for the sake of showing the variety of ways that applicants can speak about themselves and their experiences while responding to UC prompts. These essays offer an additional opportunity for critique and application of concepts discussed in this chapter.

Politics Applicant Response to Prompt #1

> I can't remember exactly when I decided to go back to school, but I do remember the night when I realized that I needed to. I was twenty-four, sitting in a bar with a friend who was in law school. We were meeting a

friend of hers who had just graduated. She and I were in the middle of a pretty heated debate over whatever was in the news that day. Her friend showed up and after introductions I asked him what he thought, fully expecting to be vindicated. I wasn't. In about a five-minute period he showed me how ignorant I really was. He tried to explain why I was wrong, starting with historical examples, read the confusion on my face, switched to macroeconomic theory, saw that I wasn't following, and finally switched to the philosophical justifications. He even threw in some formal logic, although I didn't know it at the time. Looking back, I realized that he was trying to find some area of study that I could understand. He was pretty nice about it, but by the time he finally trailed off, I made a quick escape to the bar feeling like I had been punched. The night just went downhill from there. I have always been a voracious reader, but I had never heard of the authors my companions were discussing. I've always followed the news, but I couldn't analyze current events in a critical way. That was the night that I learned that both Iran and Iraq had been British colonies, as well as India and Pakistan.

 I've always been interested in politics, in the interplay between people and divergent interests and in the process by which hard decisions are made. I realized that night that my interest was shallow and politics is about analyzing vast amounts of information and reading the subtext of world events not simply watching TV and absorbing what the pundits say. If I wanted to study politics I would need those critical thinking skills.

 I've taken every political science class offered at my community college. I didn't want to spend my last semester without any political science classes so I lobbied the department to run a " Current Issues in International Relations" class which will be part of the curriculum next semester. I'm currently working with my professor to develop the course syllabus. I've had to research and analyze what will be the emergent issues in the world over the next twenty years by critically looking at the news and understanding what issues underlie the stories being reported. I've had to learn how to strike a balance between the amount of information out there and what can realistically be covered in one semester. Developing this course has taught me how to take my personal bias out of the issues and present them fairly so that the course material would be accessible to all students (Community College Transfer Applicant to the UC).

One more paragraph follows in this essay. It does mention that the student participates in his college's student government, but that discussion doesn't add significantly because it is so general.

That this student uses his humility as motivation to keep learning rather than giving up is striking. Instructors are grateful for students who are mature enough to acknowledge their own ignorance and open-minded enough to admit that a first opinion can be wrong. Examples in this essay cause me to believe in and respect this student's passion for politics and critical thinking. That he has the initiative, responsibility, and dedication to work with a professor to institute a new class in his discipline and develop that course's curriculum is icing on the cake!

Medical Anthropology Applicant's Response to Prompt #1:

My decision to major in anthropology was one that required a long path of academic interests and a great deal of soul searching. However, my interests in anthropology began after visiting the Smithsonian at age 8. By 12 I had acquired such a fascination with the Amish that I decided that I wanted to live with them for a year to experience and understand their way of life. When I revealed my desire I was informed that it had a name – Anthropology.

As my personal anthropological adventures continued into studies of Goodall, Kroeber, Fossey and Mead, other important areas of my life's interests were developing. I began to explore the world of activism and social justice work that I felt was in keeping with my Quaker heritage. I started volunteering at the Resource Center for Non-Violence and took on two causes-- abolishing the death penalty and ensuring women's reproductive rights. In 1995 I participated in an American Friends Service Committee workshop on the Pine Ridge Lakota Reservation in South Dakota, enhancing my anthropological perspective.

I started at [community college], at age 15, dabbling in many different areas of interests. I fell in love with most of them, particularly human biology. To further explore this world of study I took a job at age 16, as a dental assistant. At 19 I began interning for a local herbalist. I thought I had found my chosen path. I was great at biology and found it fascinating.

However, something was missing – humanity. I needed the human face to the biology classes I loved and the honest extension of human understanding that seemed to be missing between doctor and patient – and furthermore, didn't the world need those things? So the struggle between my love for science and humanities began. I couldn't decide between the 2 and agonized over having to choose my major. In the meantime, I formed 2 clubs at [community college] – the Student Unity for Global Justice Club, and it's offshoot, the Communication Club. Both clubs were geared at initiating dialogue between the student body that not only coordinated cross-curricular themes, but used the themes to help us understand the functioning of the world at large. These clubs helped me to see that the subjects we study in school cannot be separated when applied to life. We cannot discuss injustices such as the AIDS crisis in South Africa and Haiti without discussing the biological implications of inequality.

It wasn't until I had done a two year balancing act between science and humanity, with my club activities acting as scales, that I rediscovered anthropology as a unifying force for my passions. In an Anthropology of Religion course I was introduced to the concept of medical anthropology. It was like a bell rang between my ears announcing that the perfect major train had just pulled up to the platform, and I held the ticket to board. I embarked on a mission to complete the anthropology series at [community college]. Everything fell into place. Choosing anthropology has reshaped my life in a way that allowed me to combine my passions.

    I am currently involved in Culture Shock – the College's Anthropology Collective – absorbing the works of medical anthropologists Paul Farmer of Harvard University and Nancy Scheper Hughes of UC Berkley. I am also serving on the student senate this year in an attempt to educate myself on the political process of making change and it has been a rewarding opportunity to serve the school that has served me so well. Having had this political, scientific and cultural experience of education has given me insight into my future academic goals. These include attending UC Berkeley and then going to pursue a doctorate in medical anthropology so that I can utilize the knowledge I have accumulated to advance this field of research and educate others on the importance of culture and medicine. (Community College Transfer Applicant to the UC)

Precocious and curious--those are the first impressions I get of this applicant. The introduction effectively informs us what is to come in the rest of the essay.

Self-guided research shows initiative. Solid examples of volunteer activities in line with Quaker beliefs suggest integrity. However, the connection of some of the volunteer activities to the academic goal is not made clear (prompt #1 asks specifically about this connection). The essay also misses the opportunity to show how the applicant fulfilled responsibilities, developed or demonstrated skills, or even the length or degree of her commitment to the volunteer work. This reads a little too much like a list. Perhaps some of the volunteer work could have been addressed better in the response to Prompt #2, along with an expanded discussion of what was gained from the experiences and why they were pursued.

Some of the work addressed controversial issues (such as abolishing the death penalty and protecting women's reproductive rights), but the presentation of this is not preachy and, therefore, would not likely offend university readers. A discussion of *how* the Lakota experience helped the anthropological perspective was missing. However, the author appears open to exploring interests in order to make informed decisions. After all, the applicant began working as a dental assistant at age 16 and interning with an herbalist at 19. Purposefulness is an asset in the pursuit of higher education.

The exploration of the writer's perceived dichotomy of academic interests, and later its resolution, reveals a capacity for self-reflection. In addition, I trust that the applicant understands and appreciates the nature of the study of medical anthropology.

This applicant's grasp of the interdisciplinary and multidimensional nature of a strong undergraduate education suggests that this transfer student may be a natural scholar. The example of the AIDS crisis makes an impressive point that illustrates the applicant's ability to think analytically.

The essay is not without its weaknesses, however. The depth of description of the founding of the two clubs would have been more appropriate in a response to the second prompt. The mention of the goal of attending UC Berkeley in the personal statement is unnecessary, but the earlier reference to studying the work of UCB faculty makes such mention more relevant than it would otherwise be.

Greater description of the relationship between medical anthropology and social change would enhance the conclusion. The struggle to embrace both science and humanity could also work as an introductory discussion. Such a change might facilitate the flow of the author's story--a chronological format is not always the most effective.

The statement contains some writing errors, but they are not deal-breakers. Did this student respond to the prompt? Does the applicant convey a sense of initiative, motivation, and dedication to education (mentioned in the rationale) with adequate description and detail? My answer is "yes."

Medical Anthropology Applicant Response to Prompt #2:

> My approach to education has always been one of full participation and integration of academic spheres. I am an extremely involved learner – using my classroom abilities in conjunction with my passion for understanding life to create a proactive learning environment for myself, my fellow students, and community. I love campus life. I feel it is always a place where our minds are particularly open to new ideas and ways of seeing. The potential of this excites me. I feel that extracurricular activities are integral to the completion of a good education. I have been actively involved on my campus through my work with the Student Union for Global Justice, Communication Club, Anthropology Club, and Student Senate. I have also been fully involved with intra-curricular work. I spent a winter session semester studying Spanish in Oaxaca, Mexico where I was able to immerse myself in the curricular learning as well as enhance my education through first hand experience with another culture. I will be completing the anthropology series at [community college] next semester and complementing my studies with some volunteer work at a local archeological dig. If I am admitted to the University of California my level of educational involvement will only grow with the added opportunities that come with a four-year University.

This essay would be even more persuasive if instead of listing so many activities, the applicant went into greater depth regarding involvement in a few of them. The introduction supports the student's claim of a comprehensive approach to education. However, there is minimal discussion of how the applicant benefited from involvement in the activities. The student does not mention here that she *founded* two of the clubs at the community college, but she should--prompt #2 is where such a discussion belongs. There is minimal description of the applicant's role and applied skills regarding club involvement and the student senate. I do gain a sense that this student takes a proactive approach to life and seeks out new and varied experiences. The claim that the UC system will provide an even richer range of opportunities is relevant and, consequently, refreshing. The weaknesses in writing are rare and insignificant enough that they should not cause a problem.

Medical Anthropology Applicant Response to Prompt #3:

> My first two years at [the community college] were very difficult and transitory for me. After graduating from an alternative high school, I started community college at age 15. That same year my father left my mother and I. The emotional impact of his leaving was tremendous on me. Not only did I have to learn how to father myself, but now I had the added economic responsibility of helping my mother with her antique business – as that had become the sole wage earning entity for our family. While this situation absolutely affected my academic performance at [the community college], I learned a lot about independence. It took me a while to find a working balance, but I was eventually able to stabilize my school life. In fact, my schoolwork became more and more important to the stability of my own life. School was where I found my passion despite my early challenges. I was able to obtain an overall UC G.P.A. of 3.94. The satisfaction comes from knowing that I did it on my own, despite the pressures that I learned to deal with so young. The experience has given me the confidence in myself with which I muster now to joyfully ask you for the opportunity to challenge myself with a UC education.

Despite some weaknesses in writing and the trite ending, this response underscores the applicant's resiliency and self-direction. The writer wisely gives only enough detail about the hardship for the rest of the story to make sense. What is most emphasized is the transformation of a difficult family experience into one that became personally productive. It is easy to believe the claims that the student cultivated a sense of independence and stability from embracing college studies. Although the GPA is identified elsewhere in the application, the writer underscores a new message by mentioning it in the context of this essay: that the challenge was, indeed, overcome and that any weak term in the academic history should be overlooked because it does not accurately reflect true potential. These points are not stated directly, but through the story as a whole.

International Politics Applicant Response to Prompt #1

> The importance of understanding other people's cultures was drilled into me by my mother when I was young. At age ten, I was given the opportunity to visit my relatives in Vietnam. The abject poverty I witnessed was a culture shock. I watched children searching for food, and thought, "How could these people who have so little have defeated my rich, powerful nation?"
> While I was in Saigon, I visited a Vietnam War museum. I saw pictures of the victorious Viet Cong taking Americans prisoner. There was also an old MIG fighter with American flags painted on the fuselage, each flag symbolizing an American plane that had been shot down. I was

shocked that someone would take pride in shooting down an American airplane---"Weren't we the good guys?"

Years later, I would be reminded of that experience in comprehending international relations, as I listened to former Secretary of Defense, Robert MacNamara, speak of the need to "empathize with your enemy". Dr. MacNamara reiterated the point my mother taught me, that Americans were viewed as the French imperialists were before them. The Vietnamese people saw the Vietnam War as a war of liberation, not of world communist domination, as the Americans viewed it. I then understood the significance of studying a people's history and culture first-hand, in order to understand their current actions in the context of international relations. Eventually I saw that the studies of history and culture compliment each other. I am traveling to Oaxaca, Mexico this winter to continue my exposure to other cultures.

I also developed an interest in the use of military force, and how it affected international relations. My mother tempered my new interest by telling me stories of what it was like living in a war zone. She instilled in me the importance of striving for a peaceful solution first. I was again reminded of Dr. MacNamara's words, as he remorsefully looked back on his role in the Vietnam War, and urged future policy makers to use military force "proportionally", not use all the force at one's disposal if the result of using that force was unethical. After listening to Dr. MacNamara, and studying the failure of U.S. foreign policy in Vietnam, I am now convinced of the importance of showing restraint and using force proportionally.

As I grew older, I began to search for a greater meaning in all the history I was studying. I asked myself if there was a greater cause in which I could use what I learned to make a difference. I found that the history I had researched tied into the discipline of international relations. As I read through the centuries, the past became the present, and I awoke from my studies to realize that I had a solid understanding of the current world security environment.

During my freshmen year of college, I attended the Model United Nations Far West Conference, and was a representative to the committee that dealt with international security. I negotiated and passed a resolution on curbing international terrorism. The process of negotiating with other delegates showed me the significance of fostering international cooperation in order to obtain collective security. The experience also taught me that I had a talent for negotiation. It was then that I decided I wanted to major in Political Science or International Relations.

I have concluded that this is where I am needed. In the words of Teddy Roosevelt, I can "spend myself in a worthy cause." I hope to use my education to help prevent unnecessary conflicts, and provide collective security to both my country and the world (Community College Transfer Applicant to the UC).

The primary strength of this statement is the depth of understanding of the topics discussed. This is communicated through a variety of technical examples—commentary on concepts presented by a former secretary of defense, experience at a mock United Nations event, and provocative discussions with Mother. The applicant thoughtfully analyzes each of these examples and even makes connections between them so readers gain a clear understanding of the complexity of this applicant's thinking process. The depth of this essay could not have been "faked" by someone lacking in dedication to his academic discipline.

European History Applicant Response to Prompt #1

A helpful critique of this essay would consider prompt #1's rationale and would compare the readers' sense of the applicant with the impressions gained from other prompt #1 responses.

> My intended major is European History. My earliest and most formative years were spent in the suburbs of Washington D.C. during the late '60s and early '70s. It was there and then that my deep interest in history and society developed. My parents were very liberal, Kennedy-style Democrats who instilled their children with the social ideals of the Civil rights Movement and their sources in American history. As a family we frequently visited many sites and monuments the D.C.-Maryland-Virginia area.
>
> In school, as soon as I could read, I devoured books on U.S. History, and I remember many field trips to Washington where current history was being made. Against the backdrop of the Vietnam War and the Civil Rights Movement, I formed my lifelong passion for history.
>
> Through my knowledge of history, I am able to place the events and experiences of my world in perspective. My understanding of the sciences, literature, religion, politics—in short, all the creative, inventive, inquisitive fields of human endeavors—are palpably enhanced by the stories of their origins and development.

This is an adequate essay, but it offers many opportunities for improvement. Its strongest, most descriptive point is the applicant's grasp of the role of history in the broader world and the nature of history as interdisciplinary. However, none of the essay's content *clearly* relates to the writer's experiences as an adult. The applicant leaves readers wondering if he has visited sites of historical interest on his own as an adult and where and how *European* history comes into the picture. He could have highlighted a specific historian or book and gone into depth about how he was influenced by that—beyond having his passion fed. In declaring that his knowledge of history enables him to place events in perspective, he could have given a specific example. Such additions would have further revealed *how* this student thinks and would have conveyed an impression of him as an active learner instead of a passive one. This essay lacks the depth of many other essays.

European History Applicant Response to Prompt #2

In 1989, I went to Stuttgart, Germany to enroll in a course designed to prepare Movement Education teachers for state-approved jobs in Waldorf Schools. The three year, full-time course was given in German, and included pedagogy and curriculum, anatomy, art and movement courses.

Upon graduation, I took a position as an English/Movement teacher at a K-12 Waldorf school near Hamburg Germany, where I stayed for the next two years.

These five years had an incredible impact on my life. I learned a new language and culture and made lifelong friends and associates.

Complete immersion in German society was difficult and lonely at times. But it gave me flexibility and confidence. I gained new capacities along with a new profession. It deepened my understanding of people, helping me to connect and relate to others of different ages and backgrounds.

My interest in European History springs from this desire to connect and communicate with people separated by languages and customs. I want to explore new ways to learn about the things that we share as members of a global community. My five years abroad will help me to do just that.

Greater cohesion would have benefited this essay. The description of the curriculum, aside from that it was taught it German, is not relevant to the theme of the applicant's potential to contribute to the university. Greater depth and more descriptive examples, of how the applicant's understanding of people was deepened, for instance would enhance this essay's impact.

Note the difference between the following essays that respond to prompt #2 regarding experiences with the Model United Nations Program.

First Model U.N. Response to Prompt #2

During my sophomore year of college, I was selected to represent China on the Security Council, at the Model United Nations Far West conference. My teammates and I trained all semester, learning about our country's history, and honing our negotiating skills in mock sessions. After arriving at the conference, these skills proved to be invaluable, as coalition building became essential to successfully passing my country's resolution.

Because of budget cuts [at my college], this year's…Model United Nations class was eliminated. So I founded the Model United Nations Club so that [my college] would still have representation at the conference. My ability to negotiate helped me gain the necessary votes on the Student Senate to approve funding for the Model United Nations Club.

As President of the…California College Republicans [at my campus], I have found my proficiency in negotiating to be invaluable in setting debate terms with the Democratic Club. I imagine that similar situations will occur when I transfer to the University of California. I will bring my ability to effectively negotiate with others to the Student Government and California College Republicans of the University of California. After obtaining my PhD, it is my hope to put my negotiating talent to work in helping to prevent conflicts from occurring (Community College Transfer Applicant to the UC).

Second Model U.N. Response to Prompt #2

I am very dedicated to projects I believe in, and pursue projects with an intense focus. The Model UN conference I attended last year is one of my most valuable college experiences. It gave substance to what I've been studying and convinced me that politics is exactly where I want to be. I was crushed when I found out that the administration wasn't going to run the class again this year citing budget reasons. The Model UN is too valuable a program to let die. I, along with two former Model UN students, have worked tirelessly to make sure [our college] would be represented at the Model UN conference this year. We formed a club, which I am the vice president of, and sought and received funding from the student senate in order to sponsor a country at the conference. Our next step is to write a proposal showing the importance of this program to take in front of both the student and faculty senates, and once the proposal is passed, we will take it to the [college] administration and ask them to bring back this class with full funding. This dedication and teamwork is what I bring to the University of California (Community College Transfer Applicant to the UC).

Both are effective essays, mostly because each has one primary topic and uses descriptive examples accompanied by in-depth observations. The first student underscores his negotiation and debate skills while the second emphasizes teamwork and dedication.

Applicants often fear that their essays will lack originality if the subject matter itself is not distinct. For purposes of admission to the UC, however, originality is more a matter of the angle that each student takes rather than in the topics chosen. Unique themes are refreshing, but if they are overly contrived they will fail to convey the information requested. I appreciate the comparison of these two essays as an illustration of distinct perspectives on a similar experience (Community College Transfer Applicant to the UC).

Family Hardship Response to Prompt #3

As the sixth of seven children raised by a single mother, I am blessed with the love and camraderie of my siblings. Through the financial setbacks my family faced, we learned to support one another and to work together in order to overcome hardships. The first memory I have of my father was while visiting him in prison. I was only three years old. Throughout my childhood he seemed to come in and out of our lives sporadically. Since my father had no viable way to support our family, we lived a nomadic existence. Before I had reached high school, I had attended ten elementary schools.

    The instability of my childhood has inspired me to build my own future. The desire to overcome such adversity burns inside me vehemently. This motivation has allowed me to simultaneously support myself while achieving academic excellence. While growing up my father used to tell me that I was a "winner." Whether or not I believed him at the time, I learned to "roll with the punches" life seemed to throw at me. I am confident that my ability to persevere despite distractions and setbacks will carry me far in life.

    The simplicity of this essay and its concise summary of hardship without self-pity make it believable. The second paragraph could benefit from one or two more detailed examples, but in the context of the information that precedes it, it succeeds in conveying an upbeat tone of success.

    The errors in the text (camaraderie is misspelled and more space is needed after the period that ends the sentence with the last word "prison") would have been caught by computerized spelling and grammar programs. If this type of error had appeared in the applicant's other essays, too, I would be concerned.

Chapter 3
Essays and Scholarships

Scholarships, like financial aid, can be confusing. A scholarship is the form of financial aid most likely to require an essay for selection, so some explanation is necessary here.

Scholarship money, unlike money from loans, does not need to be repaid. Private and public universities; individual UC campuses; and alumni, professional, service and community organizations all offer scholarships. Scholarship amounts, eligibility and application requirements, deadlines, and essay instructions vary. Scholarships can be based on financial need, academic performance, community and volunteer service, academic discipline, type of employer, re-entry status, ethnicity, or other criteria determined by the funding sources. University applications often contain lists of and information about university scholarships. Scholarships from other funding sources can be identified via financial aid offices, professional and community organizations, the internet, and books in college, career, or transfer center libraries.

I discussed scholarships with the following UC personnel:

- Garrett Naiman, Scholars Program Coordinator, UCSB
- Cheryl Perazzo, Scholarship Coordinator at UCSC
- Mary Coronado, Scholarship Coordinator, UCR
- Judith Frank, Assistant Director, Financial Aid Office, UCB
- Shawn Brick, Student Financial Support, UCOP
- Cathy Pickett, Scholarship Coordinator, UCD

I asked the following questions:

- What are the scholarship committee members looking for in the personal statements of transfer students? Do you know if and how this differs from what is looked for by admissions staff?
- Is there any difference between what is looked for in the personal statements of first-year applicants and those of transfer applicants?
- Generally speaking, the UC campus admissions representatives with whom I've spoken have said that applicants are not penalized for writing that is not strong. Is the quality of writing in the personal statement more important in the selection of scholarship recipients?

Transfer applicants can make sure they are considered for appropriate scholarships by correctly and completely filling out the financial aid and scholarship sections of the UC application. In some situations, applicants are then mailed supplemental information and instructions. Often, the UC application, including the personal statement, is all the material that is needed for review by the scholarship committees.

Types of UC Scholarships

Some scholarships are granted on the basis of financial need and GPA. At some campuses, selection for this type of award does not involve essay review; at others, essays are important. Other scholarships are merit- or academically-based. For these, personal statement essays are usually weighed heavily, as is the quality of writing. Scholarship committee members, who review applications and read essays are typically faculty, administrators and financial aid officers. Committee composition varies by campus.

Unfortunately, some UC campuses offer no scholarships for transfer students or offer only a few through their Transfer or Re-entry offices. Consequently, transfer students who are hoping to pay for their university education with the aid of scholarship money should verify that the transfer campuses they choose do offer scholarships. This way, transfer applicants are not limited to applying to off-campus organizations for assistance. However, applicants are encouraged to apply to off-campus sources of scholarships, as well.

Other UC campuses do award scholarships to transfer students. Usually, first-year and transfer applicants are in separate application pools for separate scholarship awards. As a result, transfer applicant personal statements are not typically compared with those of freshmen/women.

Scholarship Essay Content

While reading essays, committee members for the most competitive academically-based scholarships tend to look for clarity of thought, writing and critical thinking skills, imagination, focus both in writing and in life choices, and indications of the potential for success. Cheryl Perazzo, Scholarship Coordinator at UCSC, affirms that transfer students, with their greater and more varied life experience, often have an easier time demonstrating the potential to succeed.

In the selection of recipients of scholarships based on financial need, only *some* of the following should be apparent in the essays: evidence of potential to succeed, strong desire for education, writing skills, clear life focus, and evidence of having overcome challenges. Given that only some of the above need to be demonstrated, personal hardship (other than financial need) is *not* pivotal! Typically, English as a second language is taken into account in essays that are part of need-based application.

Alumni scholarship committees tend to emphasize leadership, initiative, and the context in which the applicants have achieved success. On private university scholarship committees, meanwhile, members are more likely to seek out evidence in the essays of a match between the applicants' values and the values espoused by the stated university mission.

The following excerpt from an actual transfer personal statement not only illustrates an effective response to question #1, it was used successfully as part of a scholarship application.

Throughout my youth, I spent a great deal of time exploring wilderness areas in both Canada and the United States. As a result of these experiences, I developed an interest in the interrelatedness of biological communities and an awareness of the serious challenges facing humanity with regards to our relationship with the environment. I decided to seek the necessary skills that would allow me to actively participate in identifying and implementing the means of resolving complex environmental problems. Obtaining a degree in conservation biology is an important part of achieving this objective. In order to complement my academics, I have sought out activities which provide me with hands on experience in biology, and which offer opportunities to contribute to my community.

From the Fall of 2002 to the Summer of 2003 I served as a volunteer naturalist intern at ____ Park. Under the supervision of the Parks Crew Leader, I helped design and implement an informational database for the numerous plant species that live within the park. The database can be accessed by both park visitors and staff through the city's website. The website provides images and detailed information about each species, allowing for easy identification of plants in the field. In the Spring of 2003, I was recognized by the City Council as an outstanding volunteer for my work on this project.

In the last year, I have spent much time volunteering at a national estuarine reserve. The slough is one of the few relatively undisturbed coastal wetlands remaining in California, providing research opportunities in fields such as ecology, behavior, and restoration. During the first half of 2003, I participated in their Raptor Monitoring Program. The acting research coordinator trained me on techniques for the identification and field observation of various raptor species. I was entrusted with 3 objectives; first, to monitor known raptor nesting sites; second, to identify previously unknown nesting sites; and third, to construct a periscopic device that would allow for the unobtrusive viewing of nest boxes. The highlight of these activities was my discovery of two mating pairs of white-tailed kites. Over several months, I made detailed observations of their mating and nesting behaviors, and witnessed the fledging of their young.

For the Fall 2003 and Spring 2004 semesters, I am undertaking an independent research project as a cooperative effort between my community college and the reserve. With guidance from the research coordinator and a professor of plant biology, I am designing and implementing a series of experiments to determine how oak and eucalyptus stands influence the development and growth of understory plants. The results of my investigation will be used in the formulation of land management priorities for the Reserve. (Community College Transfer Student Admitted to the UC)

The applicant uses the essay to reveal relevant and impressive information about himself. For scholarship purposes, the statement also conveys clarity of thought, writing and critical thinking skills, imagination, focus both in writing and in life choices, and indications of the potential for success. Recognition as an outstanding volunteer, construction of a new device and the undertaking of independent research all project these traits.

Readers gain other supplemental information about this student. He has exposed himself to a variety of tasks related to his field: the design of a computer database, implementation of field research, construction of a device to facilitate scientific research, and creation and supervision of experiments. The biological subjects of his work include both plants and animals. In summary, this transfer student has revealed that he understands and is receptive to many aspects of work in his field.

The fact that both a professional researcher and a professor are willing to sponsor and oversee his independent research project is a strong vote of confidence that this transfer applicant is already capable of university level work. Finally, he has followed through on his stated goal of contributing to his community, a good indication he would contribute to a university community, too.

Readers are able to extract this crucial information because the writer has indeed provided adequate description of his most relevant experiences. If he had simply listed the places he had volunteered, as many applicants do, we would know significantly less about him. He would have been less likely to stand out as a three-dimensional person.

This essay also demonstrates a common shortcoming. The main way it could be improved would be with the addition of some discussion of what the student gained from his experiences. It is possible to infer based on his descriptions, but inferences can be mistaken. It is important not to challenge the admissions or scholarship readers to infer anything. If those responsible for selecting students have to read into an essay, they are working too hard. Question #1 asks applicants to explore what they have gained from their experiences. This exploration should be part of any response to this prompt.

This transfer student was ultimately chosen as a recipient of a prestigious $20,000 UC campus scholarship.

Other Considerations

Scholarship applicants who are asked to submit supplemental personal statement essays in addition to, or instead of, those required for admission, are advised to follow the exact instructions and speak directly and completely to the specified topics. Too many scholarship applicants don't get the money they seek because they submit an essay written for one purpose and set of instructions as they apply for an award that requires an essay based on distinct instructions and topics. Time spent on the completion of a new essay may save applicants a lot of time in the future by making it unnecessary for them to work while they are at the university, so the extra effort is worthwhile.

Chapter 4
Private and Out-of-State Universities

As great as the variation is in the weight, role and other considerations of the UC transfer application essay among different campuses, it is even greater for private and out-of state universities and four-year colleges (in brief, *public* institutions of higher education are funded largely by tax money designated by the state; *private* institutions are largely funded by sources other than public monies, such as religious organizations and alumni).

In California, the *public* California State University (CSU) system does not require a personal statement for admission to undergraduate study (study in pursuit of a Bachelor's degree), but the *public* UC system does. Public universities in other states are similarly inconsistent. *Private*, vocational (job-specific) colleges are the most likely private institutions to admit students without requiring essays. In contrast, the majority of private, liberal arts (broad-based educational) universities in all states *do* require essays as part of the application process.

Although such variation and the huge number of universities around the nation makes it difficult to give information about every institution's use of the transfer essay in its selection process, I do want to offer some guidance to California community college students who are transferring out-of-state or to private four-year schools.

Private Universities and Four-Year Colleges

One factor that can be counted on among private universities is the high value that is placed on strong writing in transfer essays. In addition, private universities typically do want applicants to explain their choices of university. This should be done, as much as possible, with information of substance about each specific university as it relates to the applicant goals. Transfer students, especially, should be able to refer knowledgeably to instructors and areas of specialization, publications, and research or to unique opportunities that pertain to their own academic interests. Most college Web sites provide links to faculty pages that reveal some of this information. Detailed exploration of college Web sites or well-planned visits to campuses should uncover distinct opportunities and resources.

Otherwise, there is a great lack of consistency regarding essay considerations among private universities. Essay topics range tremendously in content, seriousness of tone and opportunity for creativity. Similarly, essay lengths and instructions vary. Some universities ask for as many as five essays, some allow applicants to choose topics from as many as six options, some limit responses to as few as 200 words, and others allow submission of essays of up to 2000 words. Most private schools require *transfer* applicants to write an additional essay describing academic goals and explaining how they think the institution will help them reach those goals. In order to save time and effort, applicants often try to use an essay written for one institution to apply to a different one that has other instructions and topics. Even if the instructions or topics seem only minimally different, applicants should write separate essays for all colleges. They should follow instructions exactly and make sure that they are addressing each separate prompt. The following examples underscore the diversity of essay topics and requirements of private institutions.

University of Chicago

The University of Chicago's Web site has extensive detailed information regarding transfer requirements and application. According to the site (http://www.uchicago.edu), the university places great emphasis on the application essays. Transfer applicants are asked to explain briefly how they believe the University of Chicago provides a specific kind of educational opportunity that corresponds to the applicants' own objectives and the reasons for transfer. Applicants are then asked to speak separately and briefly about their favorite cultural or intellectual work. Finally, applicants must write a third essay, longer in length, on one of five topics. The options range from prompts as fanciful as jumbo-sized grocery items to others as intellectually complex as how language, including personal speaking patterns, distinguish people. Students are encouraged to respond as creatively, lightly, or seriously as they wish. This school's approach is so free-style that further guidance is superfluous.

University of Southern California

The University of Southern California (USC) requires all applicants to write 500 to 700 words about either of two intellectual topics (a specified quote by Mahatma Gandhi, or an intellectual, creative, or scientific work chosen by the applicant). Transfer applicants also write one paragraph in response to each of three topics: an experience or accomplishment and what was learned from it, how USC can facilitate the exploration of each applicant's academic interests, and the reasons for transfer to USC.

I asked Kirk Brennan, Senior Associate Director of Admission at USC, to speak about his observations of transfer essays. He emphasized the importance of honesty in essay responses—he mentions that a phrase like "warts and all" was once considered for inclusion in the instructions. USC wants to know that transfer students conduct their lives with a sense of intention, are ready to commit to a major quickly, write well, and are ready for *full-time* study at a demanding university. Admissions folks expect to see a clear sense of self and direction from transfer applicants. USC appreciates that transfer students often give high priority and value to their education. Brennan is disappointed that the most common shortcoming in transfer essays is weak writing. Brennan cautions applicants about being overly-creative—he does not like to see content that is so quirky that it detracts from conveying a sense of who the writer is or content that is so over-dramatized that it calls into question its authenticity. No content should be included simply for shock value! It is important that USC understand why applicants want to study there. Although "success at USC depends on strong writing skills," Brennan also believes many ESL students may be overly concerned about the issue of language in the essays. He points out that USC has a large international population and that admissions professionals "understand the tone of ESL essays."

As with UC personal statements, a discussion of hardship is not required for a powerful essay. Nor should standing out be considered the most important objective of the essay. Greater emphasis should be placed on outcomes of experiences than on unnecessary details of the experiences themselves. Brennan encourages homemakers to focus on what they will bring to campus in discussions that draw from their experiences during time away from college.

In general, selection decisions are made by admissions staff. Academic preparation and performance are more important in selection of transfer students than are essays, which are not assigned specific weight.

Santa Clara University

After Santa Clara University (SCU) asks applicants to explain briefly how they know of SCU and why it is one of the schools to which they are applying, it asks for one to three page essays that are more creative and personal in tone. Applicants may choose to write about one of five topics and are asked to do so in the spirit of the Hawaiian tradition of "talk story." Applicants select between the topics of an unforgettable experience, a moving discussion, a pivotal turning point, an actual ethical dilemma, or an inspirational person.

I interviewed Sandra Hayes, Dean of Undergraduate Admissions at Santa Clara University (SCU), who initially surprised me by saying that although intellectual ability exhibited in the essays is never a bad thing, it is *not* the first thing for which SCU is looking. Dean Hayes explains that while many other components of the application can reveal intellect, only the essay can give a sense of the applicant as a whole person outside the classroom. This sense of person is the primary factor that SCU seeks during essay review.

SCU expects reflection from transfer students that is more sophisticated than what is typically seen from first-year applicants. Dean Hayes comments that transfer applicants often understand the use of the essay as a tool better than do high school applicants, but the quality of their writing is too often poor. Re-entry students should explain the timing of their return to college. Although Hayes acknowledges that some ESL students may struggle more and complete more drafts of their essays, the writing level of the end result is usually good enough. Applicants need not stretch to include discussion of hardship in their responses. Hayes comments, "Not everyone comes with baggage and this is not a bad thing! Applicants don't have to dig deep and stretch for something they think will be riveting."

Although Catholic Jesuit thought is interwoven throughout the SCU curriculum (SCU is a religiously affiliated university), Dean Hayes explains that applicants need not avoid controversial topics or opinions in their essays as long as they "allow the reader to know that they've given a lot of thought to the issues and are open to further exploration." SCU is a great place to explore world religions and views, Dean Hayes affirms, and instructors invite balanced conversations. Applicants to religiously affiliated colleges often wonder how much they need to discuss their own spiritual beliefs in their application statements. This, too, varies by institution, but Sandra Hayes is eager to make clear that applicants to SCU need not be Catholic and that students who aren't Catholic are comfortable at USC. Indeed, SCU admissions professionals are not looking for any reference to spiritual practice in essay content! *After* an offer of admission is extended, applicants have the option of self-reporting about their religious preferences. Of those who have recently reported, 55% reported a Catholic preference. Hayes further explains that more relevant than religious affiliation may be students' interests in social justice issues because social justice is the theme that recurs most in SCU curriculum.

Out-Of-State Four-Year Colleges and Universities

Variation in application essay topics and instructions holds throughout the United States. Public out-of-state universities often ask transfer students to respond to different essay questions than are posed to first-year applicants. At least one of the transfer essay questions typically asks applicants to explain why they are leaving their most recent colleges to transfer to the specified universities. This is the case with the University of Massachusetts (Umass), the University of Virginia (UVA), and the University of North Carolina (UNC), for instance. Transfer applicants UMass are also asked to write fewer than 500 words to explain life experiences they want the admissions officers to understand (http://www.umass.edu). At UVA, also a public institution, transfer students are usually asked to choose their additional prompt from a different (though sometimes overlapping) set of questions than those from which high school applicants choose. UVA transfers are asked to write a short and longer essay. Typically, the additional essay topics are creative, such as writing a response to a conceptually provocative quote. At UNC, the additional question pertains to how the transfer applicant can contribute to campus life. UNC asks for a 250-word response to this question. It also offers an optional question (also calling for a 250-word answer) regarding exceptional talents or challenges and programs and activities of import. Most public universities outside of California weigh transfer academic performance and preparation more heavily than transfer essays, too.

According to Senior Assistant Director of Admissions at UNC, Rebecca Edwards, UNC reads all transfer applicant essays. Like admissions professionals at the UC, UNC readers look for explanations of academic histories. They also strive to extract from the essays a solid sense of each applicant's personality. At UNC, the transfer essays carry less weight than do high school applicant essays. Although they are less important than academic performance and preparation, well-written transfer essays can be instrumental in facilitating the selection of transfer applicants. Essay review does take into account the quality of writing. Ms. Edwards has noticed that transfer applicants are more likely to submit a hastily written essay than are first-year applicants. Although this can work against them, Ms. Edwards clarifies that transfer applicants aren't likely to be denied admissions based solely on essays they submit.

ESL students can be at a disadvantage if the quality of their writing calls into question their ability to succeed at UNC, but admissions officers actively search through a variety of indicators for verification that these students can succeed in classes taught in English. The evaluation of ESL applications takes into account many considerations including the quality of the writing in the essay, English composition grades, TOEFL

(Test of English as a Foreign Language) and AP (Advanced Placement) scores, and the length of time the applicants have lived in the U.S. and how they have been spending that time.

Ms. Edwards has noticed that some applicants who have been homemakers present themselves as apologetic or dull. This should be avoided! Homemakers are not necessarily at a disadvantage in applying. They have to draw from their experiences to convey, through strong writing, their potential to contribute to the university community.

Edwards confirms that even essays that lack stories of life-changing experiences can be great. One of her favorite essays was written about an applicant's big feet! The essay was informative while it entertained.

Like Rebecca Edwards, UVA's Dean of Transfer, Greg Roberts, likes risk-taking and unusual opinions presented in essays. Although he wants to be entertained, he cautions people who aren't funny against using their essays to try to be so. He cautions people with strong opinions to show factual bases for their opinions and refrain from dogmatism. During our interview, Dean Roberts identified a few common essay shortcomings: a lack of adequate specificity, unsupported generalizations, and writing so poor that it buries the applicants' voices. He characterizes boasting as repetitive, subjective, and aggressive. He appreciates that transfer essays are more likely to cover a broader range of subject matter and recount more powerful life stories than are typical of first-year applicant essays. Like the other public universities I've discussed, UVA weighs transfer academic records more highly than transfer essays.

Students should be sensitive to the differences between universities in the use of transfer essays and in essay topics and instructions. Applicants demonstrate their respect for universities by customizing their essays accordingly.

Chapter 5
Recommended Resources

Community College Resources

The University of California provides training to community college counselors at conferences each academic year. Usually, each conference includes a workshop on admissions essays. In addition, some campus-specific workshops make mention of the personal statement. This training, as well as extensive experience, makes college academic counselors a great resource for transfer students who are writing their application statements. California community colleges employ general academic counselors but often assign some counselors to specific programs such as Puente, MESA, EOP&S and transfer and other college centers. Consequently, students can usually find counselors in a range of places on community college campuses. Universities send admissions counselors to some community colleges to conduct counseling sessions with potential applicants. Students should ask their transfer centers about such visits because they may be able to have their essay drafts reviewed by actual admissions counselors from the universities of their choice, an opportunity not usually available any other way.

Teaching faculty are often flattered when students ask for their assistance in reviewing drafts of personal statements. As busy as they are, instructors often make time for this task. They've had to write such statements themselves and, most likely, asked for help from others as they did so. Teaching at the college level requires a high level of proficiency in writing, so instructors should be knowledgeable helpers.

Many community colleges have writing centers staffed with trained tutors and instructors. Such writing center personnel see countless application essays each fall. They have been able to compare and contrast essays to gain a sense of what is and what is not effective. Of course, they are experts on the rules of writing as well.

Online and Corporate Resources

Although the number of online and corporate resources available to help application essay writers is increasing rapidly, there are still none that specifically target the questions raised by transfer students. In addition, admissions professionals insist that such resources are more likely to use formulaic templates as models. College readers are wary of any assistance that is so great or detailed that it dilutes or replaces an applicant's authentic voice. Some admissions professionals worry that the for-profit nature of online and corporate resources encourages such over-involvement.

I spoke with Kathleen Martin of Kaplan Inc.'s Undergraduate College Consulting Program who is adamant that Kaplan consultants do not use templates or write any portion of client essays. According to Ms. Martin, Kaplan's feedback to applicants:

> Regards grammar, flow, tone, and structure...[Consultants] don't even write or suggest sentences. [They] will call attention to areas needing help. [Essay consultation] starts with a conversation in which the consultant asks the customer to tell about him/herself. The consultant listens for potential revelatory stories and usable moments and anecdotes and looks for a "light bulb" moment regarding applicant goals and/or desire to attend college. The applicant writes a draft and delivers it to the consultant during the next meeting usually scheduled for no more than a week later. The average number of revisions is four to six. The enrollment agreement specifies that the Kaplan consultant will never contact the target school directly and won't write the essay. The consultants use a word-editing feature on the computer. Their work is monitored in this way.

Essay guidance is only one possible use of Kaplan's undergraduate application guidance services. Customers buy one of the standard packages of consultation hours that can be used for any aspect of the application or decision-making process. Time can be used to address financial aid questions or parental concerns, for instance, but is measured and limited. Ms. Martin explains:

> The essay goes back and forth an indefinite number of times, until the applicant feels satisfied or time constraints are met. The consultant helps the customer manage the time and makes suggestions about what might need more or less time.

Distinct from the Undergraduate College Consulting Program, Kaplan's Essay Review Service has historically provided review of essays used in application to graduate and professional programs. The more limited, and less expensive, review focuses entirely on grammar and typing. A more extensive and costly review also covers flow and content.

Ms. Martin claims that few *transfer* students request the assistance of Kaplan's Undergraduate Admissions Consulting Program or Essay Review Service. She theorizes that transfer applicants may have more confidence and experience and, therefore, less need for such services. The costs of services provided by Kaplan and other companies (such as Princeton Review) that traditionally focus on test preparation and other admissions resources are prohibitive for many students, however. High school seniors with parents who can afford to pay for college educations at elite institutions are also more likely to be able to afford the assistance of private admissions guidance companies. Transfer students as a group may be less able to afford such assistance. Although transfer applicants may be advised that both Kaplan and Princeton Review offer some scholarships for some services, they should be cautioned that transfer- specific expertise may be limited.

Like the services offered by office-based for-profit essay review businesses, online essay services raise questions among many university admissions professionals. Suspicions persist regarding templates and authenticity of applicant voice. Again, price may be prohibitive to many applicants and transfer-specific information is likely lacking.

EssayEdge.com, a CyberEdit Network Site (http://essayedge.com), provides, for a fee, guidance to applicants to undergraduate, graduate, and professional educational programs. The homepage explains, "Our 200+ **Harvard-educated** editors do not merely offer critiques and proofing; they also provide superior editing and admissions consulting, giving you an edge over hundreds of applicants with comparable academic credentials." A number of university admissions administrators have questioned the meaning of "Harvard-educated." Nevertheless, EssayEdge.com offers a course that explores specific common questions, provides essays to review as examples, and grants an opportunity to ask questions of consultants.

Printed Resources

General Essay Guidance

Ginsburg Gill, Nancy. The Subject is You: Writing the Transfer Essay. N.p.: Foothill College Writing Center, n.d.

> This outstanding guide has not been widely distributed, but should be accessible by contacting the Writing Center at Foothill Community College. The book acknowledges the dearth of guidance for transfer students regarding transfer application essays. Ginsburg Gill's background is apparent in her focus on excellence in writing and her thorough discussions of writing techniques and considerations. She includes a section on essays written for purposes other than applications, such as English class assignments. The author's examples reflect an understanding of issues specific to transfer students. Sample personal statements reveal in-depth academic exploration beyond that which can usually be pursued in most high schools. This text is limited only by the number of sources on which the research was based. Admissions professionals at three of the nine campuses of the University of California were consulted. In addition, the UC personal statement requirements referenced in the guide are different from those that are currently in use.

Mason, Michael James. How to Write a Winning College Application Essay. 4th ed. N.p.: Prima, 2000.

> While this is another general guide about application essays, the chapter on scholarship essays is a refreshing addition. I was pleased that the collection of sample essays includes weak essays, too. Understanding critiques of weak essays is as instructive as understanding those of strong ones.

Staff of the Princeton Review. College Essays that Made a Difference. New York: The Princeton Review, 2003.

>This book immediately identifies the intended audience as high school applicants to highly selective colleges. Authentic essays represent students from extremely diverse backgrounds. No critiques are provided. A chart of punctuation and grammar rules, with examples, is helpful for applicants at any level of higher education. Admissions staff at thirteen prestigious schools answer questions including "what experience would you like students to write about more often?" and "what's the most ridiculous essay topic you've seen?" Answers are presented according to college. The book confirms the variety of preferences among admissions staff. An index of essay themes is useful. Transfer issues are not addressed.

Underrepresented Students

Black, Isaac. African American Student's College Guide. New York: Wiley, 2000.

>This is a useful resource for African American students. Discussions of how to cope with issues such as having experienced a poor period in one's history may prove helpful to other transfer students as well. The book includes a chapter for transfer students as well as a section on application essays with corresponding critiques. Not only does the book cover some rarely addressed themes such as the advantages and disadvantages of attending traditionally black and predominantly white colleges, it also offers data and refers to other helpful organizations. The author provides a list, with explanations, of top colleges for African American students, as well as a chapter called "Black Arts: Colleges of Art, Film, and the Performing Arts." The discussion of financial aid and resources is detailed.

Mark. "How to Get Your Share of the $90 Billion Scholarship Jackpot." Ebony Sept. 2003: p83A, Johnson Publishing Co.

>While this article mentions essays only in passing, it is the best summary I've seen regarding the pursuit of scholarships. It lists some lesser known sources for "free" money, such as labor unions. An eleven-page listing of scholarship programs is oriented towards African American and minority students. It offers data including targeted disciplines, contact information, and award amounts. The text acknowledges a variety of applicant circumstances common in any population of transfer students. As an example, the article tells the story of a mother who chooses to wait to attend college until after her children are all in school themselves.

Shiskoff, Muriel M. Dream Catchers: A Transfer Guide for Native American College Students. Irvine: Center for Educational Partnerships, UCI, 1999.

This college orientation manual for Native American transfer students is excellent. Shishkoff's explanations of issues such as accreditation, major preparation, and impacted status are helpful to any community college student intending to transfer. Specific information about Tribal Colleges is included.

United States. Dept. of Education. <u>Preparandose a Tiempo para la Universidad: Un Manual para los Padres de Alumnos que Cursan la Escuela Intermedia</u>. N.p.: U.S. Dept. of Education, 1997 <**http://www.ed.gov/pubs/GRFC Span/grfspan.html**>
This pamphlet was prepared by the U.S. government during the Clinton administration for Spanish-speaking parents of high school students. This downloadable resource seeks to facilitate the recruitment of Latino college students by educating their parents. Bilingual transfer students may benefit from this pamphlet if they are first generation college students or if their monolingual parents are involved in relevant decision-making. No mention is made of the application process, but information about specific resources and organizations is offered. Test preparation, especially relevant to private school admissions, and an orientation to financial aid, are helpful although the financial aid details are likely outdated.

University Sources

Regents of the University of California. "UCnotes/Application." <u>UCnotes</u> Sept. 2003. Oakland: Regents of the University of California <http://www.ucop.edu/pathways/ucnotes/september03/app2.html>.

The University of California itself compiled and distributed this two-page pamphlet so the document has the great advantage of providing information straight from the source. Not only does this handout include actual personal statement instructions and topics, it also explains the reasons for the recent change in prompts and format as well as the rationale behind each prompt. While most of the information is available in the application itself, some of it, including quotes from Susan Wilbur, director of Undergraduate Admissions, provides helpful context. Community college students can also get this pamphlet from counselors and transfer centers.

University of California, Berkeley, College of Engineering. <u>Personal Statement for the UC Berkeley College of Engineering Admission Application</u>. Berkeley, California: University of California at Berkeley, College of Engineering Student Affairs Office, 1999.

This handout provides a breakdown of additional specific questions to be answered in response to what is now Question #1 of the personal statement section of the UC application. Students interested in UC Berkeley's College of Engineering cannot go wrong in consulting this concise document.

University of California, Berkeley's Office of Undergraduate Admissions. <u>Transfer Admission</u>. Berkeley: UC Berkeley Office of Undergraduate Admissions, 2003.

This pamphlet offers detailed guidance beyond what is provided about the personal statement in the UC application. One page of the pamphlet's six is devoted to the topic. Some reference is made to private and out-of-state institutions of higher education. The pamphlet specifically focuses on concerns of transfer students. Much of the information is helpful to applicants to other UC campuses as well.

University of California. UC Gateways. 2004.
https://www.ucgateways.org/index.cfm?fuseaction=content.showpage&MN=262&level1=4&level2=2&level3=0

This web page provides a tutorial for writing the UC personal statement specifically. The content is directed towards high school senior applicants, but preparatory exercises and guidance regarding the short essay format will help transfer applicants as well.

Writing

Judd, Karen. Copyediting: A Practical Guide. 3rd ed. Menlo Park: Crisp, 2001.

Essay writers would do well to check their own writing by making use of this reference. The index is exceptionally thorough, detailed, and easy to use. Listed items are as specific as the use of who and whom, commonly misused words, and spacing.

Merriam-Webster's Concise Handbook for Writers. 2nd ed. Springfield, Mass.: Merriam-Webster, 1998.

An easy-to-use table of contents begins this guidebook for writers. Clear explanations are provided throughout the text. Each point is accompanied by numerous examples, including those of exceptional, less obvious circumstances. Sections covering the use of dashes, hyphens, and colons—devices often used in essays—are thorough. This is one of the more affordable guides as well.

Complete Works Consulted

Anonymous. Phone interview. 5 May 2004.

Anonymous. Phone interview. 10 May 2004.

Akagi, Kathryn. Phone interview. 4 May 2004.

Black, Isaac. African American Student's College Guide. New York: Wiley, 2000.

Bonous-Hammarth, Marguerite. Phone interview. 25 November 2003.

Brennan, Kirk. Phone interview. 26 November 2003.

Brick, Shawn. E-mail interview. 24 November 2003.

Brown, Lena. Phone interview. 9 December 2003.

Burnett, Pamela. Personal interview. 23 October 2003.

California Postsecondary Education Commission (CPEC). "Your Portal to Education Beyond High School." 2003 <http://www.cpec.ca.gov/>

College Entrance Exam Board. The College Handbook for Transfer Students. 3rd ed. New York: College Entrance Exam Board, 1993.

Coronado, Mary. E-mail interview. 5 December 2003.

Dang, Michael. Personal interview. 5 November 2003.

Davidson, W. and S. McCloskey. Writing a Winning College Application Essay. Princeton: Peterson's, 1996.

Edwards, Rebecca. Phone interview. 27 July 2004.

Ehrenhaft, George. Writing A Successful College Application Essay. 3rd ed. Baron's Educational Series. New York: Barons, 2000.

EssayEdge.com: A CyberEdit Network Site. 2004<http://www.essayedge.com> EssayEdge's Harvard Editors. "Tips on Writing the Admissions Essay." EssayEdge.com: The Net's Admissions Essay Resource. n.p.: EssayEdge.com, n.d.<http://www.essayedge.com>.

Evans, Nathan. Phone interview. 6 November 2003.

Ewers, Justin. "The Admissions Maze." U.S. News & World Report 1 Sept. 2003: 64+.

Fauroat, Susan. Personal interview. 5 November 2003.

Frank, Judith. E-mail interview. 5 December 2003.

Ginsburg Gill, Nancy. The Subject is You: Writing the Transfer Essay. N.p.: Foothill College Writing Center, n.d.

Giomi, Robert. Personal interview. 21 October 2003.

Greene, Howard R. and Matthew W. Green. Presenting Yourself Successfully to Colleges. New York: Harper Collins, 2001.

Hayden, Thomas C. The Insider's Guide to College Admissions. Princeton: Peterson's. 1999.

Hayes, Sandra. Personal interview. 12 February 2004.

Hsu, Caroline. "An Advisor Speaks." U.S. News & World Report 1 Sept. 2003, 73+.

Jones, Lori. Personal interview. 5 November 2003.

Judd, Karen. Copyediting: A Practical Guide. 3rd. ed. Menlo Park: Crisp, 2001.

Kaplan Test Prep and Admissions. 2004 <http://www.kaptest.com>.

Koch, Nadine and K. William Wasson. The Transfer Student's Guide to the College Experience. Boston: Houghton Mifflin, 2002.

Lopez-Zavala, J. Jesus. Personal interview. 27 April 2004.

Lundgren, LaRae. Phone interview. 30 October 2003.

Mark. "How to Get Your share of the $90 billion Scholarship Jackpot." Ebony Sept. 2003: p83A Johnson Publishing Co.

Martfeld, Julie. Email interview. 11 December 2003.

Martin, Kathleen. Phone interview. 24 October 2003.

Mason, Michael James. How to Write a Winning College Application Essay. 4th ed. N.p.: Prima, 2000.

Matthews, Jay. "The New College Game." Newsweek 1 Sept. 2003: 40+

McCawley, Michael. Personal interview. 4 November 2003.

Mekis, Donna. Phone interview. 10 December 2003.

Merriam-Webster's Concise Handbook for Writers. 2nd ed. Springfield, Mass.: Merriam-Webster, 1998.

Myers McGinty, Sarah. The College Application Essay. New York: College Entrance Exam Board, 1997.

Naiman, Garrett. Phone interview. 5 February 2004.

Nannini, Daniel L. Navigating Your Way to Successful Transfer to the University of California. 1st ed. Culver City: DLN, 2002.

Parrett, Tera. Phone interview. 14 May 2004.

Perazzo, Cheryl. Phone interview. 5 December 2003.

Pickett, Cathy. E-mail interview. 5 December 2003.

Regents of the University of California. "UCnotes/Application." UCnotes Sept. 2003. Oakland: Regents of the University of California <http://www.ucop.edu/pathways/ucnotes/september03/app2.html>.

Roberts, Greg. Phone interview. 22 July 2004.

Ruiz, Encarnacion. Personal interview. 5 November 2003.

Shiskoff, Muriel M. Dream Catchers: A Transfer Guide for Native American College Students. Irvine: Center for Educational Partnerships, U.C.I., 1999.

Slayton-Mitchell, Joyce. Winning the Heart of the College Admissions Dean. Berkeley: TenSpeed, 2001.

Staff of the Princeton Review. College Essays that Made a Difference. New York: The Princeton Review, 2003.

Steinberg, Jacques. The Gatekeepers: Inside the Admissions Process of A Premier College. New York: Penguin, 2002.

Stelzer, Richard. How to Write a Winning Personal Statement for Graduate and Professional School. 3rd ed. N.p.: Petersons, 1997.

Stewart, Mark Alan and Cynthia C. Muchnick. <u>The Best College Admission Essays</u>. New York: Macmillan, 1997.

---. <u>Perfect Personal Statement: Law, Business, Medical, Graduate School</u>. 2nd ed. N.p.: Peterson's, 2002.

Swann, Claire and Stanley Henderson. <u>Handbook for the College Admissions Profession</u>. Westport: Greenwood, 1998.

"Undergraduate Application." <u>University of California: It Starts Here</u>. 2004. University Of California. 13 February, 2004 <http://www.universityofcalifornia.edu/admissions/undergradapp/welcome.html.>

United States. Dept. of Education. <u>Preparandose a Tiempo para la Universidad: Un Manual para los Padres de Alumnos que Cursan la Escuela Intermedia</u>. N.p.: U.S. Dept. of Education, 1997 <http://www.ed.gov/pubs/GRFC Span/grfspan.html>

United States. Dept. of Finance. "2004-2005 Governor's Budget Summary: Higher Education." <u>Welcome to California: State Budget</u>. 2003 <http://www.dof.ca.gov/html/Budgt04-05/BudgetSum04/04-05_BudSum.htm>

University of California, Berkeley, College of Engineering. <u>Personal Statement for the UC Berkeley College of Engineering Admission Application</u>. Berkeley: University of California at Berkeley, College of Engineering Student Affairs Office, 1999.

University of California, Berkeley's Office of Undergraduate Admissions. <u>Transfer Admission</u>. Berkeley: University of California, Berkeley Office of Undergraduate Admissions, 2003.

University of California. UC Gateways. 2004. https://www.ucgateways.org/index.cfm?fuseaction=content.showpage&MN=262&level1=4&level2=2&level3=0

Van Raalte, Susan D. <u>College Applications and Essays</u>. 4th ed. United States: Arco, 2001.

Vernon, James R. <u>The Role of Judgment in Admissions</u>. Diss. RAND University, 1996. Santa Monica: RAND, 1996.

Villasenor, Victor. Personal interview. 28 October 2003.

Wilbur, Susan. Personal interview. 21 October 2003.

Woods, Geraldine. <u>College Admission Essays for Dummies</u>. Indianapolis: Wiley, n.d.

Annotated Bibliography

Black, Isaac. <u>African American Student's College Guide</u>. New York: Wiley, 2000.

>This is an extremely useful resource for African American students. Discussions of how to cope with issues such as having experienced a poor period in one's history may prove helpful to other transfer students as well. The book includes a chapter for transfer students as well as a section on application essays with corresponding critiques. Not only does the book cover some rarely addressed themes such as the upsides and downsides of both traditionally black and predominantly white colleges, it also offers data and references other helpful organizations. The author provides a list, with explanations of top colleges for African American students, as well as a chapter called "Black Arts: Colleges of Art, Film, and the Performing Arts." The discussion of financial aid and resources is detailed.

California Postsecondary Education Commission (CPEC). "Your Portal to Education Beyond High School." 2003 <http://www.cpec.ca.gov/>.

>A useful website for demographic data regarding institutions of higher education in California, it also offers a college guide and information regarding legislation.

College Entrance Exam Board. <u>The College Handbook for Transfer Students</u>. 3rd ed. New York: College Entrance Exam Board, 1993.

>Oh, if only there were a more recent edition of this book! The target audience is transfer students throughout the nation. Topics such as transferring credit between institutions and checklists specifically addressing the concerns of community college and re-entry students are refreshing. Unfortunately, much of the information is outdated and inaccurate. There is only one paragraph about the essay portion of the application.

Davidson, W. and S. McCloskey. <u>Writing a Winning College Application Essay</u>. Princeton: Peterson's, 1996.

>The writing process itself dominates this manual. Although transfer students are not the target audience, they may find helpful the list of questions to ask reviewers before rewriting drafts. The section on common punctuation and grammatical mistakes offers a good summary.

Ehrenhaft, George. Writing A Successful College Application Essay. 3rd ed. Baron's Educational Series. New York: Barons, 2000.

> The content of this book for application essay writers is so immersed in the issues of high school seniors that very little of it is useful for transfer students. One of its strengths is the presentation of multiple drafts of critiqued sample essays

EssayEdge.com: A CyberEdit Network Site. 2004 <http://www.essayedge.com>.

> This online business offers guidance for writing application essays for undergraduate, graduate, and professional programs; sample "before and after" essays; consulting; critiquing and proofing. Essay guidance includes a useful exploration of how to explain blemishes in one's history. The sample critiques may provide detailed input beyond what is preferred and recommended by most UC admissions representatives. Although I found no specific mention of transfer admission, typical transfer student situations, such as having to work while in school and caring for family, are referenced occasionally.

EssayEdge's Harvard Editors. "Tips on Writing the Admissions Essay." EssayEdge.com: The Net's Admissions Essay Resource n.p.: EssayEdge.com, n.d. <http://www.essayedge.com>.

> Applicants to private schools for which there are a broad choice of essay topics benefit most from this summary. Information is presented according to the chronology of writing an essay. While the sample essay used indeed demonstrates the implementation of the article's suggestions, it is so specifically structured around a metaphor that it may be difficult for the readers to imagine any other effective structure. There is a fee for the essay review service.

Ewers, Justin. "The Admissions Maze." U.S. News & World Report 1 Sept. 2003: 64+.

> This article speaks mainly to issues of admission of high school seniors to highly competitive private colleges. Its observation most relevant to transfer students is that private institutions tend to be moving in the direction of comprehensive review of applicants; they are placing a greater emphasis on non-quantitative aspects of the application, including the essays.

Ginsburg Gill, Nancy. The Subject is You: Writing the Transfer Essay. N.p.: Foothill College Writing Center, n.d.

> This outstanding guide has not been widely distributed and can be acquired by contacting the Writing Center at Foothill Community College. The book acknowledges the dearth of guidance for transfer students regarding the writing of transfer application essays. Ginsburg Gill's background in writing is apparent in her focus on excellence in writing and her thorough discussions of writing techniques and considerations. She includes a section on essays written for purposes other than applications, such as English class assignments. The author's

examples reflect an understanding of issues specific to transfer students. Sample personal statements include essay content that suggests in-depth exploration of an academic area beyond that which can usually be pursued in most high schools. This text is limited only by the number of sources, written and human, on which the research was based. Admissions professionals at three of the ten campuses of the University of California were consulted. In addition, the UC personal statement requirements referenced in the guide are different from those that are currently used.

Greene, Howard R. and Matthew W. Green. <u>Presenting Yourself Successfully to Colleges</u>. New York: Harper Collins, 2001.

> This book proposes that applicants to college should approach the process using the same concepts that are applied to business-related marketing and presentations. One of three main sections speaks to essay writing. The discussion is geared towards high school students, especially those applying to competitive private colleges. The essay topics explored most in-depth are less applicable to transfer students to public universities. A useful preparation sheet for brainstorming is provided.

Hayden, Thomas C. <u>The Insider's Guide to College Admissions</u>. Princeton: Peterson's. 1999.

> Much of the advice contained in this guide is oriented toward high school students who are bound for private colleges. The recommendations encompass topics of choosing colleges, adjusting to the freshman year, and visiting colleges before applying. There is a chapter specifically for parents.

Hsu, Caroline. "An Advisor Speaks." <u>U.S. News & World Report</u> 1 Sept. 2003, 73+.

> Although this article primarily speaks to high school seniors, a few of its topics are relevant to transfer applicants as well. One example is the challenge of addressing a problem reflected in one's academic history. In addition, the author assures applicants that working while in school, as many transfer students do, can effectively demonstrate commitment, even if such work ruled out participation in other community or school activities. Suggestions for researching potential colleges, beyond the campus tour, are applicable to transfer student as well.

Judd, Karen. <u>Copyediting: A Practical Guide</u>. 3rd ed. Menlo Park: Crisp, 2001.

> Essay writers do well to check their own writing by making use of this reference. The index is exceptionally thorough, detailed, and easy to use. Listed items are as specific as the use of who and whom, commonly misused words, and spacing.

Kaplan Test Prep and Admissions. 2004 http://www.kaptest.com

> Kaplan has added admissions guidance to its services. Admissions packages include essay-writing consulting and critique. No mention is made of transfer.

Koch, Nadine and K. William Wasson. <u>The Transfer Student's Guide to the College Experience</u>. Boston: Houghton Mifflin, 2002.
> The intent of this book is to give transfer students an orientation to study at four-year institutions and to the distinctions between such institutions and community colleges. The bulk of the content refers to information that is helpful after transfer. However, many questions I hear frequently from community college students are addressed. These include questions about general education certification, quarter and semester systems, and how to research potential or new institutions. Discussion of the application and essay writing process is absent.

Mark. "How to Get Your Share of the $90 Billion Scholarship Jackpot." <u>Ebony</u> Sept. 2003: p83A, Johnson Publishing Co.

> While this article mentions essays only in passing, it is the best summary I've seen regarding the pursuit of scholarships. Some lesser known sources for free money, such as labor unions, are referenced. An eleven-page listing of scholarship programs is oriented towards African American and minority students. It offers data including targeted disciplines, contact information, and award amounts. The text does acknowledge a variety of applicant circumstances common in any population of transfer students. The article uses as an example the story of a mother who chooses to attend college after her children are all in school themselves, for example.

Mason, Michael James. <u>How to Write a Winning College Application Essay</u>. 4th ed. N.p.: Prima, 2000.

> While this is another general guide about application essays, the chapter on scholarship essays is a refreshing addition. I was pleased that the collection of sample essays includes weak essays, too. Understanding the critiques of weak essays is as instructive as those of strong essays.

Matthews, Jay. "The New College Game." <u>Newsweek</u> 1 Sept. 2003: 40+

> This article is as much about the tactics of mostly private institutions that want a competitive edge as it is about suggestions for applicants. Non-traditional college applicants are never mentioned. However, issues of overly-refined essays, the trend towards shorter responses, and the line between hassling and more benignly "nudging" admissions personnel apply to transfer students.

Merriam-Webster's Concise Handbook for Writers. 2nd ed. Springfield, Mass.: Merriam-Webster, 1998.

> An easy-to-use table of contents begins this guidebook for writers. Clear explanations are provided throughout the text. Each point is accompanied by numerous examples, including those of exceptional, less obvious circumstances. Sections covering the use of dashes, hyphens, and colons—devices often used in essays—are thorough. This is one of the more affordable guides as well.

Myers McGinty, Sarah. The College Application Essay. New York: College Entrance Exam Board, 1997.

> The needs of high school senior applicants to private colleges are the predominant focus of this guide. Especially useful is the chart of the number and type of essay questions used by a number of high prestige (mostly private) institutions. The book encourages the use of the essay structure most commonly taught in high schools. I question the recommendation of this five-paragraph essay format because it is less likely to convey the maturity of transfer students and the complexity of their life experiences and goals.

Nannini, Daniel L. Navigating Your Way to Successful Transfer to the University of California. 1st ed. Culver City: DLN, 2002.

> This is a one-of-a-kind guide whose audience is exclusively California community college transfer students who seek admission to the University of California. The book explains requirement policies and procedures distinct to this population. Some data, such as the minimum transfer grade point averages per campus major, change continually and is likely to be outdated. The book offers two pages about the personal statement.

Regents of the University of California. "UCnotes/Application." UCnotes Sept. 2003. Oakland: Regents of the University of California <http://www.ucop.edu/pathways/ucnotes/september03/app2.html>.

> The University of California itself compiled and distributed this two-page pamphlet. Consequently, the document has the great advantage of providing information straight from the source. Not only does this handout include the current year's actual personal statement instructions and topics, but also explains the reasons for the recent change in prompts and format as well as the rationale behind each prompt. While most of this information is available in the application itself, some of it, including quotes from Susan Wilbur, director of Undergraduate Admissions, provides helpful context. Community college students can also get this pamphlet from counselors and transfer centers.

Shiskoff, Muriel M. Dream Catchers: A Transfer Guide for Native American College Students. Irvine: Center for Educational Partnerships, UCI, 1999.

> This college orientation manual for Native American transfer students is excellent. Shishkoff's explanations of issues such as accreditation, major preparation, and impacted status are helpful to any community college student intending to transfer. Specific information about Tribal Colleges is included.

Slayton-Mitchell, Joyce. Winning the Heart of the College Admissions Dean. Berkeley: TenSpeed, 2001.

> A list of application and college-related technical terms such as "rolling admissions" and "FAFSA," is applicable to transfer students. The rest of this publication, however, is geared exclusively to younger college applicants. One section is titled "The Kid Behind the Numbers," and an entire chapter is offered for parents.

Staff of the Princeton Review. College Essays that Made a Difference. New York: The Princeton Review, 2003.

> This book immediately identifies the intended audience as high school applicants to highly selective colleges. Authentic essays represent students from extremely diverse backgrounds. No critiques are provided. A chart of punctuation and grammar rules, with examples, is helpful for applicants at any level of higher educational. Admissions staff at thirteen prestigious schools answer questions including "what experience would you like students to write about more often?" and "what's the most ridiculous essay topic you've seen?" Answers are presented according to college. The book confirms a variety of preferences among admissions staff. An index of essay themes is useful. Transfer issues are not addressed.

Steinberg, Jacques. The Gatekeepers: Inside the Admissions Process of A Premier College. New York: Penguin, 2002.

> Gatekeepers offers an engaging factual account of a journalist who shadows a charismatic admissions officer at Wesleyan University for nine months in order to better understand how selection decisions are made at private elite colleges. The author interviews applicants in order to embed their perspectives throughout the book. Essays are quoted, referenced, and analyzed throughout the text. One of the most valuable messages is the futility of trying to "outthink the process" of selection and the consequent import of using one's own judgment and instinct. In chapter 2, "Don't Send me Poems," the admissions officer acknowledges that even widely accepted unofficial rules such as "don't use gimmicks" and "don't even *mention* drugs" don't always apply. It is refreshing that the applicants are people from different regions of the country and different class and cultural

backgrounds. Although the focus of the book is entirely on the selection of high school applicants, transfer students will find that this book fills in missing context behind a typical selection process while entertaining its readers.

Stelzer, Richard. How to Write a Winning Personal Statement for Graduate and Professional School. 3rd ed. N.p.: Petersons, 1997.

While this guide attends to considerations of writing an application essay, its scope is limited to the concerns of applicants to graduate and professional programs. While some guidelines might be useful to undergraduate transfer applicants, some are misleading. Actual content of interviews with graduate program deans reassures many readers.

Stewart, Mark Alan and Cynthia C. Muchnick. The Best College Admission Essays. New York: Macmillan, 1997.

All of the sample essays in this collection are written by high school students. The essays are not critiqued. Essays are grouped by theme.

---. Perfect Personal Statement: Law, Business, Medical, Graduate School. 2nd ed. N.p.: Peterson's, 2002.

The most applicable aspect of this guide targeting graduate and professional school candidates is an emphasis on the importance of the personal nature of content and tone. Transfer applicant essays should follow this principle well.

Swann, Claire and Stanley Henderson. Handbook for the College Admissions Profession. Westport: Greenwood, 1998.

In this training text for future and current admissions officers, little mention is made of the role of the essay in admissions. Curious transfer applicants, however, can find here an orientation to the institutional and ethical context in which selection decisions are made.

United States. Dept. of Education. Preparandose a Tiempo para la Universidad: Un Manual para los Padres de Alumnos que Cursan la Escuela Intermedia. N.p.: U.S. Dept. of Education, 1997 <http://www.ed.gov/pubs/GRFC Span/grfspan.html>

This is a pamphlet prepared by the U.S. government, during the Clinton administration, for Spanish-speaking parents of high school students. This downloadable resource seeks to facilitate the recruitment of Latino college students by educating parents. Bilingual transfer students may benefit from this pamphlet if they are first generation college students and/or if their monolingual parents are involved in relevant decision-making. No mention is made of the application process, but information about specific resources and organizations is offered. Test preparation, especially relevant to private school admissions, and an orientation to financial aid are helpful. Financial aid details are likely outdated.

University of California, Berkeley, College of Engineering. <u>Personal Statement for the UC Berkeley College of Engineering Admission Application</u>. Berkeley, California: University of California at Berkeley, College of Engineering Student Affairs Office, 1999.

> This handout provides a breakdown of additional specific questions to be answered in response to what is now Question #1 of the personal statement section of the UC application. Students interested in UC Berkeley's College of Engineering cannot go wrong in consulting this concise document.

University of California, Berkeley's Office of Undergraduate Admissions. <u>Transfer Admission</u>. Berkeley: UC Berkeley Office of Undergraduate Admissions, 2003.

> This pamphlet offers detailed guidance beyond what is provided about the personal statement in the UC application. One page of the pamphlet's six is devoted to the topic. Some reference is made to private and out-of-state institutions of higher education. The pamphlet specifically focuses on concerns of transfer students. Much of the information is helpful to applicants to other UC campuses as well.

University of California. UC Gateways. 2004.
https://www.ucgateways.org/index.cfm?fuseaction=content.showpage&MN=262&level1=4&level2=2&level3=0

> This web page provides a tutorial for writing the UC personal statement specifically. The content is directed towards high school senior applicants, but preparatory exercises and guidance regarding the short essay format will help transfer applicants as well.

Van Raalte, Susan D. <u>College Applications and Essays</u>. 4th ed. United States: Arco, 2001.

> This book falls short in addressing concerns specific to transfer applicants. Some of the book refers to guidance about essays, including a chart that interprets the intent of different kinds of essay questions. The bulk of the book talks about other aspects of the application process. The chapter on electronic application is a strength.

Vernon, James R. <u>The Role of Judgment in Admissions</u>. Diss. RAND University, 1996. Santa Monica: RAND, 1996.

> Although the research conducted for this dissertation is almost ten years old and took place at only one institution, Rand Graduate School, it is of interest to note the possible relevance of some of its findings. The objective of the research was

to explore the decision-making involved in the selection of applicants for admission. Vernon found that committee members' opinions were often influenced by the opinions of others and that there was a lack of consistency of weight given to different components of the applications. It was not uncommon for committee members to disagree about the positive or negative value of various considerations.

Woods, Geraldine. College Admission Essays for Dummies. Indianapolis: Wiley, n.d.

This is a general admissions manual on essay writing that targets high school seniors. Woods presents information in an informal tone. The discussion of short answer essays is a rare find and is especially applicable to the new UC instructions.

Index

A

academic counselors, 76
academic direction, 5
    choice of major, 8, 24
academic performance
    importance of, 75
    omitting transcripts, 25
    poor early performance, 34
    temporary dip
        acknowledging, 21
        explaining, 27
        sample explanation, 61
    University of California, 4
Academic Preparation (UC question 1), 8, 9, 56, 58, 61
    UCB College of Engineering, 80
academic renewal, 30
achievements, 52
active vs. passive voice, 45
addiction and recovery (sample personal statement), 47
admission by exception, 55
admissions policy, University of California, 5
admissions process
    admission by exception, 55
    advice of UC admissions staff, 22
    bigotry, 49
    comprehensive review, 4
    computerized auto-admit program, 29
    cultural awareness, 38
    hardships and, 48
    importance of personal statements, 27
    interviews with UC staff, 22
    letters of appeal, 55
    primary indicator, 4
    role of personal statements, 5, 27
    transfer vs. first-year students, 4
    UC Berkeley, 28
        transfer admissions pamphlet, 81
    UC campuses, 5
    UC Davis, 28
    UC Irvine, 29
    UC Los Angeles, 29
    UC Merced, 29
    UC Riverside, 29
    UC San Diego, 30
    UC Santa Barbara, 29
    UC Santa Cruz, 30
African American students. *See also* ethnicity

resources, 79
age concerns (re-entry), 30
annotated bibliography, 87
answers to essay questions. *See* personal statements
answers vs. essays, 37
appealing denial, 55
application reviewers. *See* admissions process
applications. *See* admissions process *and* personal statements
arrogance in personal statements, 52, 75
assistance (recommended resources), 76
    tutors, 76
    writing centers, 76
assistance programs, 56
attention-grabbing statements, 53
authenticity of voice, 25
auto-admit program, 29
autobiography, 44

B

bad grades
    acknowledging, 21
    early in academic history, 34
    explaining, 27
    temporary, 61
bibliography, 87
big words, 54
bigotry, admissions process and, 49
bisexuality. *See* sexual orientation
Black students. *See* African American students *and* ethnicity
Board of Admissions & Relations with Schools, 5
boasting in personal statements, 52, 75
books (further reading), 78
breaks in education, 5
    financial hardship, 18
    homemakers, 17
    reasons for resuming education, 34
    re-entry students, 30

C

campuses. *See* colleges, community colleges, universities, *and* University of California
career experience. *See* work experience
Catholicism, Santa Clara University and, 73
causes (controversial topics), 50
change of major, 9
changes in UC questions, 6

Chicago, University of, 72
Chicano students. *See* Latino students *and* ethnicity
choice of major, 8, 24
choice of university, 71
chronological order, 44
College of Engineering (UC Berkeley), 28, 80
colleges
    public out-of-state, 74
    University of California. *See* University of California
community colleges
    counselors, 76
    number of students transferred, 2
    resources offered, 76
composition. *See* writing skills
comprehensive review of applications, 4
concerns of transfer students, 2
concluding sentences in personal statements, 39
contribution to campus, 14
controversial topics, 11, 50
    University of Virginia, 75
copyediting, 37, 40
    book about, 81
corporate resources, 76
counselors, 76
coursework
    explaining gaps, 27
    explaining substitutions, 27
    importance of, 54
    incomplete, admission by exception and, 55
    missing, 5
    omitting transcripts, 25
    re-entry students and, 34
    repeated, 30
creativity, 45, 53
    Santa Clara University, 73
    University of Chicago, 72
    University of Southern California, 72
    University of Virginia, 75
credits, excess, 5
critiques. *See* sample personal statements
cross-cultural experience (sample personal statement), 15
cultural awareness of admissions staff, 38
cultural experience (sample personal statement, 15
cultural identity, 48
    self vs. family, 27

D

denial of admission, letters of appeal and, 55
details to include in personal statements, 26
differences among UC campuses
    selection process, 5
Disabled Student Services, 56
disorders, mentioning in personal statements, 47
diversity experience (sample personal statement), 15
divorce, 46
DSS (Disabled Student Services), 56

E

ease of reading, 7
eating disorders, mentioning in personal statements, 47
Educational Opportunities Programs and Services, 56
eligibility
    borderline cases, 29, 30
    computerized auto-admit program, 29
    poor early performance, 34
English as second language (ESL), 37, 39
    Santa Clara University, 73
    scholarship essays, 68
    university of North Carolina, 74
    University of Southern California, 73
entertaining personal statements, 75
EOP&S, 56, 76
ESL. *See* English as second language
essay review services
    Kaplan, 77
    online, 78
    Princeton Review, 77
EssayEdge.com, 78
essays. *See* personal statements
ethnicity, 48
    cross-cultural experience (sample personal statement), 15
excess units, 5
experience
    bringing to the campus, 14
    cross-cultural (sample personal statement), 15
    expressing benefits, 9
    extracurricular activities, 5
    homemakers, 17
    lack of, 12, 16, 49
    maturity and, 24
    overcoming hardships, 46
    related to major, 8
    which to mention, 9
explanations in personal statements, 27, 33
extracurricular activities, 5, 8
    expressing benefits, 9
    lack of, 49
    relating to potential to contribute, 16
    which to mention, 9

F

family issues, 5, 65
    cultural discomfort focusing on self, 27
    first to attend college (sample personal statement), 20
    trauma (sample personal statement), 35
family responsibility
    homemakers, 17
fathers, stay-at-home. *See* homemakers
fears of re-entry students, 30
feedback from others, 37, 40
financial hardship
    sample personal statement, 18, 20
    sample personal statement, 19
    scholarship essays, 67

first choice of campus, 45
first in family to attend college (sample personal statement), 20
first sentences in personal statements, 39
fluency. See English as second language
fluency (English as second language), 39
font size, UC personal statements, 7
foreign students and fluency. See English as second language
formatting UC personal statements, 7
four-year colleges (outside California), 74
full-time vs. part-time study, 34
full-time work, benefits of, 5

G

gaps in education, 5
    financial hardship (sample personal statement), 18
    homemakers, 17
    reasons for resuming education, 34
    re-entry students, 30
GATE, 30
gay or lesbian. See sexual orientation
getting attention of reader, 53
government (student), 9
GPA. See grade point average
grade point average (GPA)
    importance of, 54
    poor early performance, 34
    temporary dip
        acknowledging, 21
        explaining, 27
        sample explanation, 61
    University of California, 4
grammar, 39
    books about, 81
Guaranteed Admissions for Transfer Enrollment, 30

H

hardship, 46, 54
    admission by exception, 55
    family emergency (sample personal statement), 35
    financial
        sample personal statement, 18, 19, 20
    health crises (sample personal statement), 35
    influence on grades, 21
    letters of appeal, 55
    Santa Clara University, 73
    weight toward admission, 48
health crises (sample personal statement), 35
help from others, 37, 40
hidden agenda, 55
high school experiences, relevance of, 34
homemakers, 17, 32, 34, 73
    apologetic tone, 75
    skills inventory, 33
homosexuality. See sexual orientation
housewives. See homemakers
humility, 52
humor, 45, 53, 75

I

illness, 47
illness of family member (sample personal statement), 35
immigrants. See also ethnicity and English as second language
    sample personal statement, 19
importance of personal statements, 27, 54
inadequate experience (fear of), 12, 16
incarceration, 51
incomplete requirements, 5
    admission by exception, 55
information (recommended resources), 76
instructions
    UC personal statements, 6
internet resources, 76
internships, 8, 9
    sample personal statement, 69
interviews
    UC admissions staff, 22
introductory sentences in personal statements, 39

J

jail time, 51
jokes, 53
justifications in personal statements, 27, 33

K

Kaplan, Inc., 77

L

lack of experience, 12, 16, 49
language skills
    English as second language, 37, 39
last sentences in personal statements, 39
Latino students. See also English as second language and ethnicity
    guide for parents, 80
layoffs, 32
leadership, 5
learning disability, 47
length of personal statements, 54
lesbian. See sexual orientation
letters of appeal, 55
life experience, 1, 14
    benefits of, 5
    homemakers, 17
    maturity and, 24
    overcoming hardships, 46
low grades
    acknowledging, 21
    early in academic history, 34
    explaining, 27
    temporary, 61

M

majors
    changed repeatedly, 9
    choice of, 5, 8, 24
    clear academic direction, 5
marginalized students, 79
Math Engineering and Science Achievement (MESA), 56
maturity of transfer students, 24
memorable personal statements, 9, 53
mentors, 27
MESA, 56, 76
Mexican students. *See* Latino students
minority students, 79
misconceptions about personal statements, 54
    importance of standing out, 53
    re-entry, 31
missing coursework, 5
mistakes. *See also* English as second language
    common shortcomings, 26
    perfection, 54
mothers, stay-at-home. *See* homemakers
myths about personal statements, 54
    importance of standing out, 53
    re-entry, 31

N

name-dropping, 46, 56
nationality. *See* ethnicity
Native American students. *See also* ethnicity
    resources, 79
new UC questions, 6

O

obstacles in life, 46
older students (re-entry), 30
omitting transcripts, 25
online professional resources, 76
open-ended question (UC question 3), 17, 61, 65
opinions. *See* controversial topics
order of information in personal statements, 44
organization
    order of information, 44
    suggestions, 44
originality, 45, 53
    Santa Clara University, 73
    University of Chicago, 72
    University of Southern California, 72
    University of Virginia, 75
out-of-state universities, 71
overcoming hardship, 46

P

paper size, UC personal statements, 7
parenthood, 5
part-time vs. full-time study, 34
passive vs. active voice, 45
perfection, 54

personal hardships. *See* hardship
personal statements
    additional books about, 78
    advice from UC staff, 22
    authenticity of voice, 25
    concern re lack of experiences, 12, 16
    considerations for transfer students, 24
    controversial topics, 11, 50
    details to include, 9, 26
    different uses at different universities, 75
    essay review services
        Kaplan, 77
        online, 78
        Princeton Review, 77
    essay vs. simple answer, 37
    fabricating material, 25
    formatting for UC, 7
    importance of, 27, 54, 75
    information sought in, 5
    length, 54
    length (UC), 7
    order of information, 44
    proofreading, 37, 40
    questions for. *See* questions
    required with application, 54
    reviewing before submission, 37, 40
        professional services, 76
    role at UC, 4
    role in selection process, 27
    samples. *See* sample personal statements
    scholarships, 67
    shortcomings, 9
    tone, 45
    transfer vs. first-year applicants, 5
    UC questions, 6. *See* questions
    weight of, 54
    word count, 54
point size, UC personal statements, 7
political views. *See* controversial topics
poor grades
    acknowledging, 21
    early in academic history, 34
    explaining in personal statements, 27
Potential to Contribute (UC question 2), 14, 60, 64, 65
poverty
    sample personal statement, 18
    sample personal statement, 19, 20
Princeton Review, 77
prison time, 51
private hardships. *See* hardship
private universities, 71
problems in life. *See* hardship
professional consultants, 76
programs, student, 56
proofreading, 37, 40
psychological disability, 56
Puente Project, 56, 76

Q

quality of writing. *See* writing skills
quarters vs. semesters, 34

queer. *See* sexual orientation
questions
    UC personal statements, 6
    UC question 1 (Academic Preparation), 8, 9, 56, 58, 61
        re-entry student, 31
        UCB College of Engineering, 80
    UC question 2 (Potential to Contribute), 14, 60, 64, 65
    UC question 3 (open-ended question), 65
    UC question 3 (open-ended), 17, 61

R

racial identity, 48
recommended resources, 76
records
    explaining substitutions, 27
    omitting transcripts, 25
recovery, 47
recovery (sample personal statement), 47
Re-entry Student Services program, 56
re-entry students, 17, 30
    sample personal statement, 31, 35
    Santa Clara University, 73
    transcript omissions, 25
reference books, 78
rehabilitation (sample personal statement), 47
rejection, letters of appeal, 55
religious background
    Santa Clara University, 73
requirements
    explaining gaps, 27
    incomplete
        admission by exception, 55
    incomplete, 5
    omitting transcripts, 25
research
    for this book, 83
    interviews about scholarships, 67
    interviews with UC staff, 22
resources, 76
    annotated bibliography, 87
responses to application questions. *See* personal statements
returning to school. *See* re-entry students
review of applications
    comprehensive, 4
review of personal statements
    before submission, 37, 40, 76
        by admissions counselors, 76
        by instructors, 76
        professional review services, 76
risky topics, 11, 50
    University of Virginia, 75
role models, 27
role of personal statements, 5, 27
    University of California, 4
    University of North Carolina, 74
rumors about personal statements. *See* myths about personal statements

S

sample personal statements
    Academic Preparation (UC question 1), 11, 31, 69
    accomplishment without boasting, 52
    addiction and recovery, 47
    breaks in education, 18
    cross-cultural experience, 15
    example of weak writing, 43
    explanation of poor performance, 61
    family hardship, 61, 65
    financial hardship, 18, 19, 20
    first in family to attend college, 20
    immigrants, 19
    internships, 69
    poverty, 18, 19, 20
    re-entry student, 31, 35
    scholarship, 69
    sexual orientation, 51
    UC question 1 (Academic Preparation), 9, 56, 58, 61
    UC question 2 (Potential to Contribute), 14, 15, 16, 60, 64, 65
    UC question 3 (open-ended), 18, 19, 20, 21, 61, 65
    weak example, 14, 63, 64
    work experience, 31
Santa Clara University, 73
scholarships, 67
    sample personal statement, 69
SCU (Santa Clara University), 73
second-guessing, 55
selection process
    admission by exception, 55
    advice of UC admissions staff, 22
    bigotry, 49
    comprehensive review, 4
    cultural awareness, 38
    hardships and, 48
    importance of personal statements, 27
    interviews with UC staff, 22
    letters of appeal, 55
    primary indicator, 4
    role of personal statements, 5, 27
    scholarships, 67
    transfer vs. first-year students, 4
    UC Berkeley, 28
    UC campuses, 5
    UC Davis, 28
    UC Irvine, 29
    UC Los Angeles, 29
    UC Merced, 29
    UC Riverside, 29
    UC San Diego, 30
    UC Santa Barbara, 29
    UC Santa Cruz, 30
self, cultural discomfort in focusing on self, 27
semesters vs. quarters, 34
sexual orientation, 48, 51
short essay format, 8, 81, 94
shortcomings, 9, 26, 75
showing off in personal statements, 52
socioeconomic challenges

sample personal statement, 19, 20
Spanish-speaking students. *See* Latino students *and* English as second language
spelling, 39
spiritual beliefs
   Santa Clara University, 73
spousal illness (sample personal statement), 35
statistics, number of students transferred, 2
stay-at-home parents. *See* homemakers
strengths of transfer student essays, 26
strengths, addressing, 52
structure
   order of information, 44
   suggestions, 44
student government, 9
student organizations
   involvement in, 8
student programs and services, 56

T

taboo topics, 11, 50
talents, 14, 52
time off from school
   financial hardship (sample personal statement), 18
   reasons for resuming education, 34
   re-entry students, 30
tone of personal statements, 45
too many units, 5
tooting one's horn, 52
tragedy. *See* trauma
transcript omission, 25
transfer centers, 76
transfer students
   choice of major, 24
   clear academic direction, 5
   common concerns, 2
   maturity, 24
   personal statements, 24
   primary admissions indicator, 4
   strengths of personal statements, 26
   UC Berkeley transfer admissions pamphlet, 81
   unerrepresented, 79
trauma, 46, 54
   admission by exception, 55
   influence on grades, 21
   letters of appeal, 55
   sample personal statement, 35
   Santa Clara University, 73
   weight toward admission, 48
tutorial, 94
tutors, 76
typeface, UC personal statements, 7

U

UC. *See* University of California
UMass, 74
UNC (University of North Carolina), 74
Undergraduate College Consulting Program (Kaplan), 77
underrepresented students, 79

units, excess, 5
universities. *See also individual listings*
   explaining your choice, 71
   outside California, 71
   private, 71
   public out-of-state, 74
University of California, 4
   admissions decisions, 4
   admissions policy, 5
   application information pamphlet, 80
   Berkeley, 28
      College of Engineering, 28, 80
      comprehensive application review, 4
      transfer admissions pamphlet, 81
   campus differences in selection, 5
   Davis, 28
      as first choice, 45
   first choice of campus, 45
   interviews with staff, 22
   Irvine, 29
      comprehensive application review, 4
   Los Angeles, 29
   Merced, 25, 29
      comprehensive application review, 4
   personal statement questions, 6
   question 1 (Academic Preparation), 8, 9, 56, 58, 61
      UCB College of Engineering, 80
   question 2 (Potential to Contribute), 14, 60, 64, 65
   question 3 (open ended), 61
   question 3 (open-ended question), 65
   question 3 (open-ended), 17
   Riverside, 29
   San Diego, 30
   Santa Barbara, 29
   Santa Cruz, 30
   scholarships, 67
University of Chicago, 72
University of Massachusetts, 74
University of North Carolina, 74
University of Southern California, 72
University of Virginia, 74
USC (University of Southern California, 72
UVA (University of Virginia), 74

V

vocabulary in personal statements, 54
volunteer work, 8

W

weaknesses of personal statements, 26, 75
weight of personal statements, 27, 54
   University of North Carolina, 74
word choice, 45, 54
word count, 54
   UC personal statements, 7
work achievement, 5
work experience, 8, 9, 32
writing centers, 76
writing skills
   example of weak writing, 43

importance, 39
list of, 39
matrix of UC opinions, 39
perfection, 54
private universities, 71
proofreading, 37, 40

re-entry students, 34
resources, 81
suggestions, 39, 44
tutors, 76
University of North Carolina, 74
writing centers, 76

ACKNOWLEDGEMENTS

I wish to thank those people whose help allowed me to get past stubborn obstacles: Karen Farrow who has gone beyond the call of duty over and over again and Matthew Siverling who pushed for the project in the right places for half a year. I am grateful to for folks whose contributions far exceeded their histories with me: Jill Schettler-Susskind for charting complicated information and Jill Zurschmeide for editing the entire manuscript on a voluntary basis even while parenting, farming and contracting. I appreciate the transfer students who have been so generous in granting me the use of their personal statements and interviews, including, but not limited to: Jason Nicholson, Carol Lee, Heather Caldwll, Ben Corman, Seven Gerdemann, Jonathan Mark, Catur Holcombe, J. Jesus Lopez Zavala, Natalie Matlock, Kathryn Akagi, and Tera Parrett. I thank California State Lieutenant Governor Cruz Bustamante. This book could not have been written without the cooperation of the admissions professionals who shared their precious time with me even though they are overworked: Susan Wilbur, Marguerite Bonous-Hammarth, Pam Burnett, Bob Giomi, Michael Dang, Nathan Evans, Sandra Hayes, Michael McCawley, LaRae Lundgren, Lena Brown, Encarnacion Ruiz, Susan Fauroat, Lori Jones, Christian Villasenor, Kirk Brennan, Rebecca Edwards and Greg Roberts. Some of the UC financial aid and scholarship coordinators granted me interviews as well: Mary Coronado, Cheryl Perazzo, Shawn Brick, Cathy Pickett, Judith Frank, and Garrett Naiman. Without your guidance, Stephen Kramer, I would have lost sleep. I thank Barbara Wald for generously reviewing my work. Julie Martfeld, thank you for making important data so accessible! Donna Mekis, Kathy Odell, Steve Pluhacek and Kathy Martin, I appreciate the time and information you gave me. I am grateful for the support and professionalism of Sylvia Winder and Georg Romero of the Cabrillo College library. There's no place I'd rather do research than at UCSC's McHenry Library, so I am fortunate it is staffed with such competent and dedicated people. The enthusiasm of strangers, many of whom are transfer graduates themselves, renewed my spirit during the hard times of the project. I am grateful towards Simon "Sparky" Sherred for giving me respite with his special spark, games of Mousetrap, inventions, tickling matches, moral support during DDR, and enjoyment of old Get Smart episodes that equals mine. I appreciate Jon "Skippy" Sherred for sharing yesterday, today and tomorrow with me--it couldn't be better. Kelly Tyler and James Von Hendy deserve thanks for tolerating my work-related babble even during vacation in Costa Rica. Kelly Tyler has again surpassed herself as the most generous friend imaginable—this time by volunteering to index the book in between graduate schoolwork and half-time technical work and a transformation into an outstanding marimba player. Rachel Strauss never fails to give brilliant advice on any subject, but also helped this project along by contributing Max and Charlie who guarantee that I maintain a proper perspective on the writing of essay guides. Sharon Pomerantz has always been there for me such that I am comfortable with my place in the world, and, luckily for me, she knows more than she wants to know about the writing process. I thank Karen Kriebel, Sara Barthol, Glenn Winship, Fritzi Wisdom, Inger Stark, Craig Brown, Cathryn Clark, Lauren DeVries, Naomi Morgenstern, Richard Emigh, and Mary Margeret Peterson for contributions that cannot be listed. Thank you, Joe Wells, for your kindness and for "getting it." Thank you, Lynn Flink, for coming through at the last minute to make things right despite your own personal busy-ness. Thanks to Café Milagro of Quepos, Costa Rica and Mr. Toots Coffee House of Capitola, California for providing superb working environments and chocolate drinks.

Authors Note:

If you would like to submit your transfer application essay for use in trainings and future editions, please send it with complete contact information (name, address, phone number, and email address) to: Marcie Wald, Cabrillo Faculty, Cabrillo College, 6500 Soquel Drive, Aptos, CA 95003. I will send you a release form to sign because I can not use essays without this informed and documented permission. I am eager to collect essays that cover issues different from those in essays already presented in this book. Thank you.

Following the guidance in this book does not guarantee admission to a university of choice.